W9-BXD-300

The MENTOR'S SPIRIT

The
MENTOR'S
SPIRIT

*Life Lessons on
Leadership and the
Art of Encouragement*

MARSHA SINETAR

St. Martin's Press ❧ *New York*

THE MENTOR'S SPIRIT: LIFE LESSONS ON LEADERSHIP AND THE ART OF ENCOURAGEMENT. Copyright © 1998 by Sinetar & Associates, Inc. Printed in the United States of America. No part of this book may be used or reproduced in any manner whatsoever without written permission except in the case of brief quotations embodied in critical articles or reviews. For information, address St. Martin's Press, 175 Fifth Avenue, New York, N.Y. 10010.

Design by Maureen Troy

Library of Congress Cataloging-in-Publication Data

Sinetar, Marsha.
    The mentor's spirit : life lessons on leadership and the art of encouragement / Marsha Sinetar.—1st ed.
       p. cm.
    Includes bibliographical references.
    ISBN 0-312-18630-4
    1. Leadership—Psychological aspects.   2. Mentoring.
3. Encouragement.   I. Title.
BF637.L4S54   1998
158'.4—dc21   98-5645
                                           CIP

First Edition: July 1998

10 9 8 7 6 5 4 3 2 1

For
Father Kevin Lynch,
with thanks

CONTENTS

The MENTOR'S SPIRIT

INTRODUCTION

———◆◆◆◆———

The mentor's spirit *is the heart's posture pervading
every healthy relationship in every family, classroom,
organization, and town.*

L ET US ACKNOWLEDGE our encouragers. We are blessed if
we have friends who love us with open arms, who suffer our
going wherever we must—in short, friends who have the mentor's spirit. Willingly they leave us at what C. S. Lewis called the
World's End, if that is our heart's desire. Somehow these encouragers influence us toward our own, distinctive life.

We seem to need *mentors*—wise and faithful guides, advisers,
or teachers—the wisdom keepers of an entire family, a sprawling
corporation, or a community. Much more, we need *the mentor's
spirit:* an unseen, affirming influence and positive energy. The
mentor's spirit is the heart's posture pervading healthy relationships in every family, classroom, organization, and town. It exists
between productive managers and subordinates and resourceful
leaders and their constituents. When the mentor's spirit is absent, we find dependency, an erosion of optimism, and impaired
problem solving. To address the specific role that mentors—and
the mentor's spirit—can play in our life, in some passages I write
autobiographically about certain collegial relationships. My life's
lessons are blessings. I'd like to pass them along.

1

If we're called into a wilderness of sorts, encouragers—not always family, not always close friends—understand our heart's longing:

> "Sir," said Caspian, "will you tell us how to undo the enchantment which holds [these people] asleep?"
>
> "I will gladly tell you that, my son," said the Old Man. "To break this enchantment you must sail to the World's End, or as near as you can come to it, and you must come back having left at least one of your company behind."
>
> "And what is to happen to that one?" asked Reepicheep.
>
> "He must go on into the utter east and never return into the world."
>
> "That is my heart's desire," said Reepicheep.[1]

A PERSONAL NOTE

I have set sail for the utter east. In this, there's been encouragement. Over the years in my capacity as author, educator, and corporate adviser, many productive mentors have crossed my path. Lovely, sometimes distant, often totally surprising friendships formed when I was a school principal in Southern California from 1974 through the 1980s. Then, under the auspices of my human resources firm, I specialized in complex change management projects. Mergers were then at their peak. It was an exhilarating era. Not until 1993 did I scale back my corporate practice to accommodate a growing desire to write.

In my youth, however, encouragements were rare and came primarily from the mentor's *spirit:* impersonal love. I mean by "impersonal" those positive forces all around us, even from dispassionate or inanimate sources like the people we don't know—poets and actors—or books and cultural icons. Through high school and college I was prematurely self-supporting, living largely on my own. I sought out mentors, but helpful, caring persons capable of empathizing with me on a deeply relevant level of experience were not readily available. Out of my loneliness and sense of being different, I searched out the mentor's spirit in everyone and everything. That habit served me well. It seems worth sharing.

The mentor's spirit animates our life. It moves us toward wholeness and authenticity. Not only individuals embody the mentor's spirit but also inanimate good—what Scripture terms "principalities of goodness"—and productive motifs. These positive influences surface as ideas of truth or beauty and as intuitions of our brightest destiny. Throughout this book I'll elaborate on these two terms—*mentor* and *the mentor's spirit*—to explore the underpinnings of what helps us, young and old alike, learn how to be, live, work, or grow. Mentors and the mentor's spirit give us the green light to become distinctive contributors within the context of our life in community.

It has gradually dawned on me that, near or far, my mentoring companions share one attribute: They are life lovers, supporters who possess *the mentor's spirit:* that productive, liberating power that heartens us to develop a bit of poetry in our self-leadership and grow into our best selves, who we were born to be. Anyone who intuits our life's essential vision or themes and somehow affirms these so that we reach out for them is an artist, an artist of encouragement.

OF MENTORS AND THE MENTOR'S SPIRIT: PHILOSOPHICAL UNDERPINNINGS

It's said that the young these days distrust the future, that they feel pessimistic about their careers and financial well-being, that suicide has increased, and that even children of six and seven years old are depressed about a raped and polluted environment. We read of gang leaders destroying whole neighborhoods. In truth, some of these young toughs are gifted, if misdirected, influencers. They possess many of the same attributes of power as corporate executives. Gang leaders are politically aware. They have a charismatic knack for attracting followers, and enviable persuasive skills. They can articulate what it takes to endure within their milieu. Although gang leaders may lead impressionable disciples astray, they provide their followers with something the wider, mainstream community does not: a mentoring relationship.

Without a sound mentoring philosophy, we may misjudge that primary bond—may concoct elaborate coaching programs. Yet these can remain lifeless systems. It's critical, before evolving new programs, that we learn to observe and use our *productive* cultural resources, assess the actual merit of ideas and influencers in our lives, and identify the mentoring traits and processes that enhance optimism, self-governance, and, therefore, life itself.

The encouragers celebrated in these pages demonstrate the mentor's spirit. You might say that their attributes, indeed their lives, bear witness to transcendent realities. For instance, they are *virtuous*—good stewards of their own and the greater good. They are *trusting and trustworthy*—faithful to a constant set of superordinate values. They are *people lovers* and unabashed lovers of life. They are *empathetic and nonjudgmental*—we feel that our mentors accept us unconditionally. They are also *authentic.* Relying on an internal compass, they figure out how to be themselves despite obstacles or shifting circumstances.

Throughout this book I'll discuss such attributes, as well as a central paradox of mentoring, while weaving into my narrative ideas about what I call the mentor's spirit. Three elements have helped order my thoughts:

- Being: The Key to Mentoring
- Stillness Invites the Mentor's Spirit
- The Leadership Links to Mentoring

I'll draw an ageless, genderless frame around the topic by proposing that we find *the mentor's spirit* everywhere: in fables and film, in art, music, and poetry, through whatever ideas and images move us toward the integrities of our heart. I'll explain why the mentor's spirit is productive, why it stimulates productive *self*-leadership (rather than dependence or imitation of others), and I'll contrast productive and unproductive mentoring. While traditional leaders may mobilize us toward shared goals and values, those with the mentor's spirit unobtrusively uplift us. Their delicacy is their art. They *whisper* our verities simply by being who they are. Alive or not, real or fictional, productive mentors turn us toward our deepest, most intimate truths by expressing theirs—not by heavy-handed pronouncements. Amplifying their joyful, audacious ability to be simply themselves, mentors support life.

WHY ALMOST ANYTHING CAN UPLIFT

Unconsciously or otherwise, we spontaneously seek out daily enrichment. If we're healthy, we notice how others endure or how forces of light overcome the dark. And who does not search for practical ways to be authentic? Each of us wants to come into his or her own as an individual within the realities of our fast-paced, globally relevant times. Never before have art and science converged as they do now to give us conceptual answers for the diverse scenarios of a wide-open, anything-goes future. Virtual offerings can and do mentor. When the *Stars Wars* trilogy was recently rereleased (after some twenty years), fans across the country lined up, eager to reunite with their larger-than-life celluloid archetypes. What were they seeking? Why did they flock to that movie? I believe that some viewers are conscious and strategic when searching for the skills and wisdom they need to navigate through the rapids of the twenty-first century.

An educator who had experienced a series of losses told me she found peace of mind with the last lines of an e.e. cummings poem.

On a radio talk show, a mother reported that her daughter, a nine-year-old Down syndrome child, viewed and *re*viewed classic, coming-of-age films of a certain era, mostly movies starring Shirley Temple. The parent concluded that her daughter, being unable to absorb information verbally, used film to comprehend the subtle mores of adolescence and to mentally rehearse acting like other young girls. No one *person* was her guide, but stories and visualizations, because they could be self-regulated and watched repeatedly, mentored her. Not only fine film embodies the mentor's spirit—any idea, image, or unseen energy that reflects or enhances life confers the mentor's spirit.

With a traditional concept of mentors, someone may think, "I want to learn a specific set of skills or attitudes from a specific individual. Where's my career blueprint? Who'll mentor me?" My approach is less passive. It's decidedly spiritual and lets us engage heart and imagination actively with whatever instructs or inspires. By suggesting that nearly anything can be a mentor—a book, a painting, or, as a friend quipped, a tree stump—I do not mean to confuse. To reiterate my definitions: a *mentor* is *a person, a guide, or a teacher—the keeper of selective wisdoms* that we hope to gain. On the other hand, *the mentor's spirit is the "almost anything" that deepens our sense of the sacred or our understanding or transmits a kind of gladness about life itself.* Furthermore, I use the phrase *the* mentor's spirit. It seems to me there is but one Spirit, one good—infinite, intelligent, and unbounded—permeating reality. An illustration of how almost anything influences us seems in order.

Not many people know that John Muir, one of America's foremost conservationists, was savagely abused in boyhood—by his own father, no less. The Scottish farmer exploited his young son, cruelly using him as a sort of indentured servant. Once Muir's father forced the lad to climb down into a well shaft with instructions to dig for water. When the water rushed in, the boy nearly drowned.[2] Until he could summon the strength to leave home, Muir turned to nature for life support. Later he would disclose to friends that he feasted in what he called "the Lord's mountain house." To John Muir, the wilderness was as healing as the gentle bedside manner of a physician is to another. He felt that, "compared with the intense purity and cordiality and beauty of Nature, the most delicate refinements and cultures of civilization are gross barbarisms."[3] Muir believed most people don't realize when they're being guided and that "men, storms, guardian angels, or sheep" can guide.[4] The universe offers sustenance, if only we have eyes to see.

THE MENTOR'S SPIRIT AS A SONGLINE

Today's relationships involve ever-widening, impersonal circles. Computers, digital telecommunication systems and global linkages coax us away from close-knit attachments into ever-wider, virtual communities. Far-off colleagues have become our intellectual neighbors. We depend on people we rarely meet for data, project help, and political influence. Perhaps we thrive on these intermittent exchanges. I, for one, am frequently buoyed up by distant associates. Something about their messages, the movement of their lives, choices, or courage motivates me and brings hope. We seem fellow voyagers of a sort—busily etching timeless, spiritual songlines into the memory of the human race.

Songlines are an ancient communication system that author Bruce Chatwin studied while traveling in outback Australia. As I understand it, the Aborigines use songlines much like we use telephones, faxes, or on-line networks. These vibrational criss-crossings move information around the continent, mark out safe spaces for journeying, send news bulletins, and even organize social life, as Chatwin explains:

> I have a vision of the Songlines stretching across the continents and ages; that wherever [people] have trodden they have left a trail of song (of which we may, now and then, catch an echo); and that these trails must reach back, in time and space, to an isolated pocket in the African savannah, where the First Man opening his mouth in defiance of the terrors that

surrounded him, shouted the opening stanza of the World Song, "I AM!"[5]

In exactly this tribal fashion, we need not meet our mentors face-to-face to learn from them or hear their news, their passions, their great "I AM!" An unseen, timeless hook-up lets us receive each other's song. In some sense, truth is our song, and mentors, leaders, and artists of encouragement are predisposed to share it. Truth wakes us up. It frees us. It stimulates our wholeness. No wonder we hunger for it. As it is written,

> O you who sit in the gardens,
> My companions are listening for your voice—
> Let me hear it![6]

PART I

BEING: THE KEY
TO MENTORING

The 1st Lesson

BEING CALLS TO BEING

———◆•×•◆———

If our mentors reflect the deepest truths of their own existence, something they impart will be worth learning.

PURE BEING IS pure power. Being is our most vital principle, our essential, animating life force. As it's said, "What you *are* speaks so loudly, I cannot hear what you say." *Being* enhances a mentor's power. Being injects a mentor with persuasiveness. Doing and having are but secondary influences. The great runner Herb Elliot once described his coach Percy Cerutty as "an oasis in the desert of my lost enthusiasm."[1] His words suggest that Cerutty's *being* uplifted and rekindled Elliot's dimming, worn-out energy. Being involves our particularity, a potency we garner through simple is-ness, but not passivity. Prayer, meditation, or mindful walks along a lonely stretch of beach are not indolent times. These etch reality into awareness, enable our seeing ourselves clearly, as in a mirror. Who has not been restored, had his or her vigor renewed, by such nondoing activities? Whenever the mentor's spirit enlivens the substrata of being, our potential for effective action accelerates.

Learning her craft, a tile setter rises to ever new levels of functional mastery. Learning to be mentors, we ascend to ever new levels of being, and somehow embody the suchness of ourselves expressively—as infinite attributes reflected from within our core. What psychologists call "is-ness"—high individual presence or actuality—liberates that fruitful energy. Whoever becomes infused with the essence of being finds functional mastery expanding. How do we accomplish this? How do we *become* persons with functional mastery, high presence, and fruitful energy? Coach Cerutty believed that a runner's eyes were like a camera that captured both the subtle and gross movements of the coach. Similarly, what we do with our attention counts. With everyday behavior, our parents, leaders, and educators imprint subtle and gross values on us. Our eyes take in what others do. Our ears take in their messages. Those who *live* their cherished values can become our guides. (Those who merely preach we tend to ignore. Or we study them for the what-not-to-be lesson.)

People we never meet influence us. The specificity of one life can provide much-needed direction. In a touching exchange, TV talk-show hosts Oprah Winfrey and Rosie O'Donnell described how, for years, they were inspired by Mary Tyler Moore's example: the character she portrayed (Mary Richards) and her professional pluck as an actress of high standards and courageous good cheer. O'Donnell credited actresses Betty Buckley and Florence Henderson with impressing her through their respective roles on *Eight Is Enough* and *The Brady Bunch*. Since O'Donnell's mother died when the star was young, she sought out positive enactments of motherhood: "I had no mom . . . and I was always looking for the mom to come in [to the story line] . . . I had this whole mother transference thing going on."[2] Given their own mentor's spirit, one imagines that today O'Donnell and Winfrey are long-distance mentors to millions. Paraphrasing something Oprah Winfrey said, their hearts seem as "big as the sun."[3] Who hasn't been uplifted through faraway or unorthodox means?

A Personal Story

There was resistance to my promotion to the position of public school principal. In 1972 only two women in our district held that spot. My teaching specialty had been the gifted student, yet from the inception of my career I aspired to broader leadership. Despite a passion for teaching, I had big dreams and was always hatching plans for novel, wide-scale pilot projects, the sort that might affect large communities of learners. The fact that these innovations worked and attracted state or federal funds and were enjoyed by students didn't automatically advance my career. One colleague counseled me "Remember, Sinetar, no one likes a smart-ass broad." Another mumbled, "Why aren't you home having babies?" Our district superintendent hesitated to promote me. He was endearing, a handsome man—playful, nattily dressed, dashing. Everyone loved him, including me. One sensed good intentions, a generous heart, and he was fair.

It was obvious that I'd unrelentingly demand advancement. Denial was my way of life: I ignored the obvious and pressed on, repeatedly scoring at the top of the shortlist. My superintendent balked for a few more months about promoting me, then gave in. The day he summoned me to his office (supposedly to offer congratulations), he nagged: "What does a gentle woman like you want with this thorny leadership job? Do you realize what you're getting into?" His questions punctured my bubble of self-satisfaction.

Naive, too baffled to respond, and nervous, I burst out laughing. Then he laughed and the tension faded. Did he enjoy his Neanderthal quips? Secretly, did he hope to shock or to test people's mettle? Despite his opening salvo, I felt that he liked and respected me. He must have sensed my admiration and affection.

Paternal tendencies and unsolicited advice aside, we got on well, and given a mutual fondness for kidding around, overall things between us relaxed. Although I was routinely summoned downtown and dressed down for some excessive innovation, I was proud to be a part of that management group, going about my job like a broker selling stock in our district's programs. That's how much I loved it.

Our leadership circle (of about 100 principals and district managers) was far ahead of its time in educational philosophy and practices. We considered ourselves a team. We *behaved* coherently, gathering together monthly in one large group to plan long-term projects and meeting weekly in smaller units to follow up and implement our plans. The four or five regional administrators to whom we principals reported were a superior senior core. They were completely human (by which I mean fun loving, imaginative, and imperfect), and their ideas were educationally superb. Strategically they orchestrated our communications—practically writing scripts for the less able communicators, while leaving alone the more talented ones. Their discerning finesse revealed a sophistication I've found lacking in many Fortune 500 environments where inarticulate number crunchers *try* to coach and motivate bright executives without empathizing with them, and whose formulaic, lifeless edicts leave everyone yawning. As an educator and change-agent, I've concluded that regimented systems and manifestos can never harvest the rich diversity of individual potential. Productive mentoring demands an educative dialogue—a real relationship of mind and heart—not canned speeches or mechanized training blueprints.

An organization is an interconnection of living beings; the more vitality each one possesses, the more vital is the collective body. In other words, corporate vitality is born of an *individuated*

dynamism. I agree with coach Cerutty that "nature hates ortho-
doxy": "Without variation, there is no evolution. Natures hates
the even-beat, unvaried movements that we see today."[4] As with
runners, so with us. *Our* uneven beat reveals our truths. Only
our genuineness harnesses vitality for creative, constructive purposes. Which brings me back to my own story.

Without inordinate pressure (and, I thought, with enormous
goodwill), my early organizational elders choreographed our district's uniform policies and responses. We weren't asked to become robots when serving the corporate good, merely expected
to use our strengths—to know what these were and amplify
them. Vince Lombardi, who meticulously orchestrated his team's
victories by attending to both individual differences *and* strategic
systems, would have approved.

As individuals I felt we were completely distinctive, not in the
least herdlike. To this day, observing some inept (or arrogant)
managers of prosperous, multinational firms, I note that compared to my old colleagues they project an amateur and immature
demeanor. "Professional" managers may sport MBA degrees
from Ivy League universities; they might be technically expert.
But they frequently lack the *being* or character structure of true
leaders. Many could learn a thing or two from my former associates about *applied* good humor, actualized compassion, and the
dignified, humane treatment of people. My public sector team-
mates were people lovers and life enthusiasts. Warts and all, they
reflected that love, and their creative leadership excited mine.
There wasn't a dried-up prune in that senior bunch. A sense of
oneness gave our district its intelligent dynamism and excellent
reputation.

That same attractive spirit infuses all healthy organizations
and all nuturing liaisons between parents and children, teachers

and students, and leaders and constituents. When absent, optimism erodes, and we find the diminution of what might be called street smarts, the knack of spotting options. If people—youngsters, too—behave stupidly, it's generally because they've been mentored stupidly or cruelly or mindlessly. Or ignored. Before any of us jumps on the linear, industrialized bandwagon of mentoring, I propose that we explore the spiritual underpinnings of healthy, productive mentoring relationships. Let's guide the young, the aging—anyone interested—to assess the quality of the advice they're given before acting on suggestions about how to work, worship, perform tasks, grow, or succeed.

Some people will pick up a book like this thinking, "I want to mentor someone." Others will pick it up thinking, "I want someone to mentor me." Each of these mind-sets is addressed, and each wish progressively fulfilled by understanding—and cultivating—the mentor's *spirit*. Imbued with a spirit of contribution to community, we labor for ideals beyond ourselves. A positive spirit reorients our conduct. No longer do we just go through the motions of service: We put our heart into each generous act. With a vital mentor's spirit, we automatically *influence* others. (It's a rare bird that does not seek encouragement, a helpful phrase, or shining reliability.) And, as later chapters discuss, with a well-developed mentor's spirit, we tend to *attract* capable mentors. Either way, the key to enhanced interpersonal outcomes resides in being.

BEING: THE ANTIDOTE TO TECHNOLOGICAL STERILITY

Many large organizations express the best of intentions. They say it's their mission to provide employees with opportunities for promotional or performance feedback. These entities devise supposedly humane policies for corporate dialogue. They want to do the "right thing." Human resource specialists create exhaustive systems, value-based and written down unequivocally, in black and white: "Every manager of every department *will* speak to every employee at least once a year. They *will* give feedback. We believe in two-way dialogue. We're a people-centered company."

Personnel departments conduct wide-scale training sessions on affirmative action or performance reviews only to discover months later that nothing's happening. A few responsible souls may tiptoe into the program, but when examining the *practices* within these organizations, rarely do we find evidenced the *spirit* of those plans—those perfectly crafted programs. Some employees wade through the murky waters of their entire working lives without ever having had so much as one decent exchange with their management.

"Human" systems need human involvement, not more technological efficiency. Without a generous spirit guiding mentoring programs, the intelligent leveraging of data and skills is retarded.

Effective mentors earn our trust if they embody whatever they deem worthwhile. Rather than preaching about honesty or fairness, productive mentors guide us toward honesty by *being* truthful when it counts. Artists of that sort may spend a lifetime trying to dig virtue out of themselves in practical actions. Even their striving nurtures us.

A friend once remarked that her mentors have all endured hard times. She's observed them move through, and survive, their grief and that has furthered her life. Their overcoming movement suggests why the mentor's spirit affirms life: Whenever we notice life resurrecting itself from a grave of desolation, we realize what's needed to be victorious ourselves. If we pay attention to the human interest stories we routinely study, our observations instruct us by providing a sort of visual guidance. For example, with mindful alertness we'll observe:

- whom we admire and why
- how others succeed
- what it costs them to survive
- what we imagine their life says to us about *our own* next steps (and, to take them, what we must improve or accept in ourselves)

Watching how another survives a trauma, the death of a loved one or an abandonment, is life-affirming—*if* we learn about life's renewal. Managing our attention, we note how others lift themselves out of despair. That can teach us to say, "I, too, can survive. I will continue—no matter what, *I am*." This is no small mentoring gift. As mentors reflect the deepest truths of their existence, something they impart will be worth learning.

As a young man, a neighbor was self-supporting. He quit school in his teens and got a job as a tree trimmer. When his older brother was dying from AIDS, local hospice workers enlisted my neighbor as a volunteer. No one person mentored him directly. He credits his work with the dying for guiding him toward his truest values.[5] His experience illustrates how society transmits its sacred values: In a spirit of oneness, we learn from each other how to live or die or sanctify our days. Today that young man is back in school, finishing a college degree in health care. The mentor's spirit touches every aspect of everyday living.

Mentoring Is a Spiritual Art

Mentoring is a timeless function. Its elements reside in our heart. In these pages I point to the traits of mentors, to a mentoring *process* and its intimate spirit. The latter transforms us in a wholistic sense: body, mind, and spirit. The word *mentoring* has mythic roots. It means "guide," as in the mythological character Mentor of Homer's *Odyssey* whom Odysseus asks to watch over the development of his son, Telemachus. As competitive social creatures, we often forget the developmental side of mentoring and may view our mentors as exploitable corporate sponsors. In that case, they become objects—power brokers from whom we want to extract some*thing,* a material or political favor. In fact, productive mentors are productive *types*—wholesome guides who, by their way of being, ignite our vision, our hope, our self-respect.

Productive mentors are found everywhere—among our closest confidants, distant mythic heroes, and archetypes. Stories and even symbols (a white dove, an eagle, a seagull) impart the mentor's spirit. Both mentors and the mentor's spirit fire up vigor of thought and zeal to reach our true purposes: inner peace, liberty, the soaring heights of some specific goal. The mentor's spirit fuels our determination to flourish as fully integrated individuals.

C. S. Lewis, Joseph Campbell, and others believed that myths encoded life teachings, truer and more substantive than any conventional instruction. From a Judeo-Christian perspective, we might view reliable mentors as outer reflections (mirrors, if you will) of some vital life force already within us. Yet it also seems helpful to accept our mentors as imperfect. If we roman-

ticize their mythic attributes or give them too much authority, we shortchange ourselves. People on pedestals tend to slip off.

BEING INCLUDES SO-CALLED IMPERFECTIONS

An old story about a spiritual master supports the last point. The master cautioned her disciples not to impose their needs for perfection on her: "You harm yourself when giving me all your power."[6]

We frequently hear of someone being disappointed by a teacher, physician, psychiatrist, or priest. Perhaps the guide or elder has been idealized or is ultra-authoritarian. When our mentors display their feet of clay, it's natural to feel betrayed. However, if we put our faith in the *spirit* of what mentors teach us, weighing and assessing the validity of their ideas, it helps lessen the tension between what we *wish* they were and what they actually are, as mortals.

If we have the luxury of working alongside our mentors, we see their flaws. This is an advantage since we can test their ideas in the circumstances of each day. Over time, we'll sort out the worth of their instruction. To suppose that our mentors are blemish-free ministering angels is to invite disappointment. No sooner do others fall short of our illusions than we cast aside their teachings—some of which could be valuable—perhaps feeling hurt and depressed in the bargain.

To utilize whatever wisdom is found, let us assess the presence of the mentor's spirit, life affirmation, in each one's way of being. Encountering others with that inner measure, we learn that almost everyone has some gift to share.

OBSERVE A PATCHWORK OF ATTRIBUTES

Again, our observational powers can secure our quilt of character. A starting point comes as we manage our attention intelligently. What are we noticing? Perhaps we'll study in others some mix of admirable attributes, habits, mannerisms, and functional styles that *we'd* like. Those qualities are already in us, if in dormant fashion. Somehow our observations let us stitch up a patchwork of traits we'd like. For instance, in an interview singer Tina Turner remarked how much she admired Jacqueline Onassis: "Her grace, her style, her intellect was how I modeled myself in terms of how I wanted to present myself off stage."[7] We may wonder what a world-famous rock star and a president's wife share in common. As she described Onassis, Turner's *own* refinement, her grace and intelligence, were abundantly evident. To me, she seemed poised, regal and royal in her own right.

Many of us direct our attention *un*consciously. No other person is precisely like us, so our growth into an individuated wholeness includes discovering the facets of being we're attracted to. Here, then, is another way that mentors inspire growth: When they're being who they are, their particularity shows *us* how to be distinctive. Another's authenticity easily inspires us to be ourselves. This is a healing benefit of simple being. Nor is it essential to be spoon-fed by our mentors. Distant, impersonal influences will do nicely.

SEEK THE MENTOR'S SPIRIT

Having struggled from childhood to harmonize certain crosscurrents within myself, such issues of leadership and mentoring hold strong appeal. Vibrant artistic and introverted spiritual drives clashed with my extrovert's wish to ennoble the world. I've needed to understand how one manages oneself or, as author Garry Wills puts it, how one mobilizes others around a shared vision. To reconcile a desire for a largely worshipful life with a yearning to enhance people's lot, I've looked not only to mentors (i.e., people) but also to the mentor's spirit. Since youth, something unseen and sublime attracted me: A divine inner image tugged at my heart and conscience. It was (I didn't know it back then) a pressing wish to merge with one great good—ultimate reality, God. Motifs of living and a discrete mode of *being* haunted me. An eternal pattern of love, not precisely any one person, summoned me as my true being. That call reinforced a spiritual ardor no individual had ever acknowledged.

Perhaps you, too, have experienced an interior tug-of-war, or have searched for friends, associates, and ideas with the mentor's spirit. Perhaps you, too, seek patterns of eternal truth that transcend "personal help." Are you quirky and independent? If so, you may shun formal mentoring, or tire of advocates who try to shape you in their own image, or get easily irked with those who pat you on the head approvingly if (and only when) you accommodate their notions of success. Free spirits, the gifted, and life lovers of every age enjoy large-hearted friends with empathy for another's hunger to be real. Mostly we read about (and occasionally we find) such open-minded gems: poets, leaders, educators—artists all and graced with the mentor's spirit. By contending they are artists all, I mean that true encouragers consciously encounter life. When mentors succeed as our personal guides, it's because they fully experience us—as we are. And vice versa.

My earliest, public sector colleagues impressed me *because* they were real. Even their mistakes (and certainly mine) were fodder for a stimulating educative discussion. We routinely dissected and analyzed our seeming errors. Problems were talked through until solutions cropped up. I don't think I ever saw the wagons circle as they do in some sectors, leaving someone out in the cold to do battle with a mishap alone. There was nothing phony or antiseptic about those talks. Some of us cried in frustration during our evaluation meetings. Others stomped out in a rage. The result of these discussions was greater clarity, the unfolding of true being. We all seemed incredibly flawed and unfinished and wonderful and, in fact, we were all growing more capable all the time.

When we look beneath the surface of appearances for whatever's real and lasting in ourselves and others, we can become capable mentors. Healthy mentoring relationships flow out of that intimate listening, that authentic encounter. Whatever failings we have, we are artists of encouragement as we relate to others genuinely and put the teeth of our values into daily conduct. It's the spirit within that mentors, as our being affirms the oneness of being.

The 2nd Lesson

VIRTUE LIBERATES BEING

———◦•×•◦———

A fundamental integrity is persuasive—the song of spirituality—and the enduring grace of goodness is what we sing about.

VIRTUE IS A mentor's most powerful tool. Virtue unlocks being. It sits on the throne of awareness. Unleashing our virtue—integrity, merit, and decency—we release pure being and that liberates others.

Here's what I mean. When we're with a virtuous person, especially a mentor or admirable associate, some of his or her positive energy flows our way. If we become aware of that vibration, we could wonder, "What is happening here? Why do I grow calm or hopeful in the presence of this individual?"

Not that we project our idealized expectations onto others or that our mentors must be blemish-free saints. Rather, our awareness of virtue invites a greater awareness of being. We'll know ourselves as more human after these productive encounters. Perhaps we'll use our mentor's virtues as patterns for our growth. Or some superabundant understanding will spill over, from his or her reflection to ours. Because it is in the nature of life to seek out and express greater life, the more virtuous our mentors, the more guiding potency they'll have. We've probably experienced what it's like to profit emotionally when around an accomplished col-

27

league. Do we also remember that our heroes and heroines—ten thousand steps removed from our lives—can affect us powerfully? I give you one example:

In his book *Second Wind,* basketball legend Bill Russell recounts long boyhood afternoons spent at the Oakland Public Library. During the lonely period after his beloved mother died, books befriended him. The library became Bill Russell's private world, a library card his "most prized possession." Russell credits one passage in a specific book for helping focus his grief and cites another favorite book, *Complete Marvels of the World,* for introducing him to a remarkable hero, Henri Christophe ("the most masterful Negro in history"), who evolved from slave to feared and powerful emperor of Haiti. Russell's passionate description of his distant influencer could remind us how remote sources have enabled our own minds to soar:

> Christophe sent chills up and down my spine. I read everything I could find about him, and every new story made him bigger in my eyes. He was shrewd . . . a monster, but he lived with such grandiose flair that I couldn't help being awed. . . .
>
> Henri Christophe was my first hero after my mother. To me he was just the opposite of a slave: *he would not be one.* He was indomitable. I think his life brought home to me for the first time that being black was not just a limiting feeling. Christophe could not be held back by anything, and his power reminded me of my mother. She too believed that anyone could command any stage; all that was required was the right style and strength.[1]

In like fashion, aspiring young golfers may identify their inborn gifts by scrutinizing a Tiger Woods. Religious girls and boys might well scour every available book about Mother Teresa's or St. Francis's early life to comprehend their own vocation. The inherent virtue in being attracts—and liberates—itself. There is a oneness about virtue, and our impersonal identifications continually show us who, and what, we are at heart.

Someone's example of fairness or nobility somehow releases those very traits in us. Goodness in another speaks to our goodness. For the religiously inclined who reflect on the life of a Cardinal Bernadin or a Dalai Lama, for aspiring photographers who mull over the career choices of an Annie Leibowitz or an Imogene Cunningham, there will come a period of asking, "Along these lines that I admire, what's possible *for me?*" That inquiry holds relevance for us. We seldom imagine our fullest potential unless our thoughts engage the "What's-possible-for-me?" inquiry while mulling over admirable ideas or individuals.

Eric Berne, M.D., the father of Transactional Analysis, called our life's program a script, conceiving of it as a theatrical production. He said that one way to decipher our script's direction is to ask, "What happens to a person like me?" Our answers provide a sense of where we are now and where we're headed and what our role entails. As wholistic mentors, we can ask our protégé, "What happens to someone like you *at your spiritual best?*" Inspiring mentors always help us resist normal lethargy or limits. If we feel hemmed into a conventional career slot, they'll challenge that thinking. Their way of being, their virtue—or power—wakes us up, motivates us, if only unconsciously. As we tell ourselves, "I'm unique in this or that way," we get unstuck, envision infinite new possibilities. Yet even within that infinitude, we'll notice our preference for a particular life, discrete values, a one-of-a-kind archetype that our mentor expresses that reflects our ultimate goal: the vivid, intelligent display of who we are, at our spiritual best.

Optimal Being as "Destiny"

We each come to our optimal futures by subtle subjective means. Somehow we blend our goals and destiny. In sum, at our spiritual best, we prefer to be *what we are*. Unhappy people always get confused about what this means. If asked, "Who are you, really?" or "What sort of life are you meant to lead?" or "What happens to someone like you at their spiritual best?" they grow unconscious or depressed. Faced with unscripted, unbounded parts of themselves, they retreat. One suspects that even those who say they fear failure frequently feel more menaced by an optimal and joyous self.

We may not *want* to believe that we have control, or a voice of authority, over our affairs, so we opt for passive, helpless modes of existence. We shy away from the responsibilities of power and self-governance, thereby undermining whatever competence we could develop. In time, our own ineptness lets us off the hook, and we sidestep guilt for our failures of nerve.

Many of us prefer to let others tell us how to accomplish things. A halfway decent mentor alters that by insisting that we learn *how* to think the high, bright thought or figure out our own solutions. Unproductive mentors hand us a sanitized to-do list— ten steps, five rules. Should we act on that, our mindless submission undermines self-reliance, responsibility, and even sours intimate relationships. By contrast, our productive guides engage us in a mature relationship. Sensitive to what's needed, they take into account such ephemeral qualities as our judgment, readiness, or immaturity. In a manner of speaking, their goal is our complete liberty—the breaking of shackles. They'll expect us to ask for what we want and trust us to live up to their trust. Both being mentored and mentoring are active, growthful experiences. Each one has a part to play. It is a myth that only elders or organizational "superiors" can be mentors. Any virtuous energy—from a friend, a child, an idea—can mentor us. To Victor Hugo's mind, even a thought was like a prayer, and "there are certain moments when, whatever the attitude of the body, the soul is on its knees."[2]

A PERSONAL STORY

After being promoted to head a prestigious school, I needed a top-notch secretary. Our student body included the children of the affluent and most of our district's board members. The community was sophisticated and well versed with sound instructional practices. The majority held advanced degrees and were leaders themselves. Many were potentially nitpickers. Our faculty was similarly talented—older and more experienced than I— and had long-standing community ties. Parents and teachers (like shareholders and employees of any corporation) exert formidable political power, especially on a principal still wet behind the ears.

Our district's grapevine had it that some school secretaries refused to work with women. School secretaries are executive assistants, a principal's alter ego. They can make or break a leadership plan. Horror stories abound. It was the early 1970s; I was new at the job *and* female and worried: What competent colleague would accept the assignment?

Good fortune reigned. One of the best *was* willing to take a chance. I liked J immediately and sensed we'd be a synergistic team. She is smart, fun-loving and glows with warmth. J empathetically yields to a child's feelings, while keeping her authority intact. Many adults involved with schools and other institutions like only children (indeed, like only *people*) who are compliant, who submissively bow to their bureaucratic powers or who appease by conforming to tidy, bootlicking norms. Not J. Nothing obstructs her vision of a child's basic dignity. Her tenderness matches theirs. Our students instantly intuited that: Goodwill radiates from J like bright light, and her virtues mentored me.

A MENTOR OF THE INJURED

In short order, our front office became a safe haven for the injured and the punished. We might as well have constructed a Statue of Liberty at our door, for countless time-out students landed on our shores: hyperactive boys (mostly), ousted from classrooms for being constitutionally unable to sit still or behave. Restlessness and academic disinterest reduced them to mischief makers or class clowns, and teachers who sorely needed a respite from the constant interruption sent these pupils to lounge in the office. It must have been a nuisance for J; every young guest required her ingenuity. She was unflappable.

Once during my first months on the job, J escorted a six-year-old towhead into my office. She presented him to me like a gift, her eyes twinkling. The child handed me a note from his teacher: "Bobby was doing 'Long Johns' in the restroom. Please handle." Long Johns, I discovered, was a euphemism for urinating into a toilet from a noteworthy distance. Alas, Bobby had missed the urinal. He'd been caught in the act by our custodian who had just mopped the tiles and was now furious. Everyone wanted the culprit punished. (Principals, like politicians, are expected to be tough on crime.) I'd never heard of this antic. It didn't strike me as a major offense, just a natural—and somewhat humorous—expression of any growing boy's self-testing. Taking the middle ground, I asked Bobby whether he'd be permitted to practice Long Johns at home. Mystified, he just shrugged. I phoned his mother to chat about the matter, quietly convincing her, and myself, that this was a totally innocent, benign occurrence and that we might injure Bobby by exaggerating its importance. She was coolheaded and like J took Long Johns in stride.

Everyone seemed satisfied: Bobby's mother, now informed, was neither shamed nor alarmed. Bobby gladly cleaned the restroom floor (thereby mollifying our concierge) and returned to class clutching my note back to his teacher. It read: "Handled." Other school secretaries might have been horrified at such mild discipline. Loving children, J understood. Her innate wisdom made our front office an ideal sanctuary for the distraught.

When unhappy or grouchy parents stormed into our office, J was the first person they encountered. She absorbed the brunt of their anger or calmed their fear. By the time they reached me, they were calmer because they'd been heard. This seems the first law of healthy human relationships: Let people speak with someone who can listen. Hearing others is also a function of being.

J stands very still and fixes her eyes on you. You know you

have the undivided attention of one who's emotionally equipped to listen to you without interrupting or impatience. After absorbing what's said, she quietly and firmly says her piece in a self-possessed fashion, and now *you* listen. (J practiced "active listening" before anyone coined a name for it.) I've never known her to overreact in a crisis. Probably her greatest challenge was managing upward: watching over the doings of her high-energy, inventive principal.

MENTORING THE CREATIVE

Out of sheer enthusiasm I generate copious amounts of work, for myself and anyone in my sphere. Early that first year I initiated a school newsletter and loved writing and sharing it. It was an instant hit, but its production involved the dreaded back and forth of endless wordsmithing. In those pre–electronic printer days, J duplicated the missive by hand. We had a monster mimeograph machine on which she'd crank out hundreds of copies monthly and stuff the envelopes and mail it all to our readership (which, due to the newsletter, was expanding). Occasionally she'd enter my office, shut the door, stand somberly in front of my desk and look me straight in the eyes to capture my full attention. Fairly brimming over with dignified self-restraint, she'd tactfully tell me to shape up. J never minced words.

I'd mend my ways: either curtail my editorial fanaticisms or shorten the newsletter or send it out less often. I rarely refused J's proposals. For one thing, she made few demands, and when she did, they were heartfelt. For another, I needed her support and valued her friendship too much to dodge her requests. I suspect that J and I loved each other in that soul-stirring, mutually respecting way that happens as people feel they're benefiting from their work together. That affection reflects the mentor's spirit.

MENTORS AS COMMUNITY STABILIZERS

Preindustrial societies leaned on mentors to stabilize community life. The mentor might be a warrior or healer, someone who understood the mystery of childbirth and facilitated the process. The wisdoms of others were entwined with daily happenings. Lucy Smith, a Dry Creek Pomo Indian, described her mother's and sister's guidance about cooperation: "We all had to live together; so we'd better learn how to get along with each other . . . I thought [my mother] was talking about us, as Indians and how we are supposed to get along. I found out later by my older sister that mother [was talking about] the plants, the animals, birds—everything on this earth. They are our relatives and we better know how to act around [them] or they'll get after us."[3]

Universally, the young look to adults for life lessons. They want to master their experiences, function well, invest in and meaningfully manage their gifts and time on earth. Youngsters wonder how to express eternal verities or contribute to their world in satisfying ways. No civilization answers such questions or develops the potential of next generations through finite, legalistic means. Prescribed, lockstep approaches are efficient and economical, but these hardly further inspired learning. Often the more gifts and sensitivities learners have, the more true dialogue (what has been called an exchange of selves) they require. These open discussions invite the reconciliation of right and wrong and further the search for answers to life's big questions. Dialogue, about which more is said later, develops that spirit of oneness mentioned earlier and helps people feel less alone. That's certainly critical to the gifted and the creative.

MENTORING THE GIFTED

Gifted girls frequently have so-called masculine interests such as powerful achievement drives.[4] To them, traditionally feminine roles may seem restrictive. Similarly, gifted boys often prefer what society labels feminine interests: art, poetry, music, dance. In fact, all giftedness transcends stereotypical categories of age or gender. For example, the creatively gifted enjoy transgenerational friendships with people both older and younger than they are. *Interests* move us all toward burgeoning wholeness, and that could take us in directions opposite to what others expect. With the creatively gifted, that flowering health usually happens sooner than later: "The higher the I.Q., the earlier the child develops a pressing need for an explanation of the universe."[5]

We assume that children with exceptional talents need special consideration and more than most. It's true that if we box these youngsters into stereotyped classifications, their potential can be squashed. However, *every* child is unique. Each one must be honored for his or her particularity. If that occurs, if adults are reasonably good stewards to the young, youngsters will be productively mentored as a matter of course rather than rubricized into subclasses.

More than many youngsters, it seemed I had ambition, big dreams. More than most adults, it seems, I love to initiate projects and pit myself against challenges. Every obstacle offers a self-test and adventure. I loved J for accepting what was then considered my inordinate drive, while she herself held to more traditional orientations of wholehearted commitment to marriage and family. I still feel her strength.

To this day, when I see corporate managers playing helpless, unable (or unwilling) to utter the simplest vision or corrective to their staff, J's forthrightness springs to mind. J is living proof that a settled disposition—quiet, inner determination—is influential. That's what I mean by *being*. Her resolve is virtue, an integrity, a spiritual trait born of authenticity and rock-solid faith in a constant set of values.

MENTORS AS SUPPORTIVE FRIENDS

Throughout a dark period of life, when I was getting divorced and was so severely grief stricken that I routinely hid in my office and wept, J was emotionally available. She consoled me without words. J may have been saddened by the breakup of my marriage, but she stood by me expressing only love. Who could forget such compassion? J illustrates the way nurturing friendships can mentor. These relationships flow from the élan vital— or being—of those who know who they are.

Paraphrasing a story that Father Anthony deMello tells, I underscore this strength: A disciple asks her master, "What must I do to attain the highest spirituality?" The elder replies, "Follow your heart, my child. Just remember that to follow your heart, you are going to need a strong constitution."[6] I include J in a tiny band of friends whose substantial constitutions befriended my life.

The appearance of each one's life has differed. My comfort came from their constancy, their spiritual strength, and the experience of being loved. Without lectures or pretense, these diverse companions exhibited hardiness. They proved to me that virtue—inner strength, cheerfulness, commitment, kindness, steadfastness—releases our virtue. When around such people, we feel a reciprocity of affection and basic decency. A fundamental integrity is persuasive. It is *the* song of spirituality, and the enduring grace of goodness is what, somehow, we sing about.

I heard once that Gandhi loved to read the Bible but refused to convert to Christianity because the Christians he met didn't embody the love they preached about so vehemently. Perhaps if Gandhi had known someone like J, he'd have reconsidered. (Perhaps not.) Anyhow, after our season of close association, I came to view the mentoring potential of all working fellowship through that experience: It is possible to love and be loved by our colleagues.

Two years after leaving the district, I became a Christian. On the Sunday of my baptism, I wished J were standing beside me in church. Her character and religious sensibilities influenced me for the better, even as these silently nudged me to abandon everything familiar for my own wilderness. Something about her goodness liberated me.

CULTIVATE SELF-TRUST

◆━◆◆◆━◆

A mentor's mentor establishes a climate of trust in which creative exploration can occur, but self-trust is an inside job.

A BLOCK TO ANYONE'S creative leadership is isolation, having no one in whom to confide. Those with drive to innovate can easily feel estranged. The capacity to venture out to the cutting edge of new ideas creates a sense of vulnerability, and every change agent needs at least one trusted colleague (and not just during troubled times). Sadly, many leaders routinely shoulder each heartache, confidence, and organizational burden alone. Even proven leaders want mentors (or at minimum friends with the mentor's spirit), in part because they're reaching into the unknown for self-expression. Mentors tend to be infused with a helpful spirit and may prefer to coach others rather than receive such favors. It's accepted that many leaders like to go it alone. A mentor of leaders establishes a climate of trust in which two-way discussions can occur. Of course *self*-trust is an inside job.

Productive mentors are congruent: They're actually who they purport to be, and that trait encourages *our* congruency. Thomas Merton once wrote that the aim of a spiritual director is simply to apprehend and support the grace that's already in each person. No matter what the context of life, if we support the worthwhile qualities within the other, we're probably mentors of some sort.

That supportive inclination is transcendent, an activity that looms above mere age, gender, personality, background, or professional title. Encouragement invites a rarified experience of self and enables us to move tangibly beyond ourselves. When people say, "I never thought I could do this, but I triumphed thanks to my parents or friends or that event," they're usually referring to some ineffable, productive influence that prodded them toward a surprising victory. That overcoming reflects the essence of things spiritual and may include accomplishing "more" or cutting back. Anything untried offers a challenge.

The mentor's spirit and productive mentors stir our inquiry, "What might it mean to grow beyond myself or transcend this supposed limit?" Our answers uncover a basic truth: obstacles present themselves to free us from supposed limits. We may *think* we can't deliver a speech or complete college or find our financial footing in life. That's our challenge: to surmount the falsity of barriers so that, on the other side of these, we're freer, know ourselves as more capable than before. Certain restrictions fall away. This is an exciting, empowering way to regard trials and it's the window through which productive leaders gaze.

Imagine Olympic athletes practicing for an event. Some elemental life-force transports them beyond their limits, above the hold of what we call "reasonable." With that same elemental energy, our mentors nudge us toward that same altitude. However commonplace a mentor's life, his or her way of *being* suggests, "To fulfill dreams, persist—don't be afraid of being a little unreasonable with yourself." Productive mentors somehow convey the notion that our stalling and stuckness often mean we are choosing comfort over growth. (Unproductive ones whisper,

"Don't work too hard, paddle about in safe shallows, avoid making waves.") Leaders run from unproductive mentors.

It's a universal phenomenon. In retrospect, we'll notice we've searched for mentors who taught us to stretch, to tolerate discomfort, to accept our high, seemingly inconvenient calling. These relationships are not all sweetness and light. Here's when the right chemistry counts. Perhaps we're attracted only to those who push us out of our comfortable cribs, thus forcing us to outgrow an infantile need for security or reassurance. Maybe something about our mentor's ambition allures us. As noted, what draws our attention probably attests to dormant qualities, alive and kicking within.

Unreasonable growth feels fragile. That's why mentors must be reliable, trustworthy. Anything most of us really want in life at first *seems* out of reach. To launch our supposedly impossible plans, we need to have well-founded confidence in those who urge us on. We also need self-confidence.

A Personal Story

A favorite colleague supported my trust of the unknown. I can't remember exactly *how* I managed to have E, our school psychologist, assigned to our faculty during my first year as a principal. (Normally new administrators get *no* favors, have no rights, and are walking targets for much teasing—perhaps like army recruits.) It was serendipitous that I worked with E, whose stabilizing perceptiveness attracts cooperation, even from those who normally shun psychologists.

My initial schoolwide objective involved a wide-scale staff-development program. Having observed continual discrepancies between what public education was and what it *could be,* my plan for improvement included developing a staff that was sincerely open to new instructional methods. Believing that a school should be a stimulating learning hub for its entire community, adults and children alike, I expected intellectual leadership from all concerned. I wanted teachers to welcome district visitors—educational experts—and to cultivate receptivity toward change. (Today, this is a given for any decent school.) Right off the bat, we designed a synergy of pilot projects: career education, cross-aged grouping, team teaching, and multicultural techniques. Limits fell away. The district's budget was restricted, yet money poured in for whatever we needed. Both parents and teachers supported the changes. Within mere months, most of us felt—and saw— the children's exuberance growing. Their excitement fed mine. To update our community about new programs, we held informal parent-education coffees in various homes. Our school quickly grew into an energized, enriched learning community, and a succession of trial-and-error accomplishments made me value everyone's empathy.

An invigorating learning hub requires trust-filled relationships. We needed to put ourselves in each other's emotional shoes. I asked E to lead an empathy training course for our entire staff: teachers, paraprofessionals, office staff, our custodian, me. In those days, that integration of personnel was unusual. However, empathy means emotional understanding and certitude. Only in-tune associates become self-sacrificing teams that proceed to cultivate victorious life skills. Trust schools self-trust.

We invited *everyone* to weekly meetings to practice active-listening skills and nonjudgmental responding. As a training site for student teachers from local universities, we urged our student teachers and parent aides to attend our training programs whenever possible. E, a master of the interactive arts, instructed, coached, and encouraged us all. I viewed our staff as an ensemble—like a chamber music quartet that must receive everyone's subtlest cues in order to perform and, through disciplined practice and inspiration, reaches collectively for the celestial note.

I'm told that others feel my desire for excellence, that that sense spurs their drive, or self-tyranny and subsequent resistance. In those days, I yearned for each teacher's heartfelt involvement in our programs and expected a no-nonsense commitment. It irked me to hear people pay lip service to ideas they thought I valued. I wanted our staff to love learning as much as I did. (Not everyone did.)

My goals typically generate joy and self-renewal in me—but not necessarily in others. I become fully absorbed in whatever interests me with an ardor akin to play. During peak creative cycles, that means living in the eye of an intensifying hurricane dominated by a commotionless, concentrated energy. When work is consciously chosen (i.e., of my own preoccupations), I am completely employed by what I do. Yeats called this engagement "a gaiety transforming all that grief." Everything (and everyone) else fades into the background. Our most talented teachers were fired up, too.

Educational experts and politicos from around the state visited to study our programs. The spotlight of attention appealed to me and to our top performers but may have distressed the less secure. (No one told me so directly.) Ours was a fast-paced environment, with rapid change our operational norm. The children took easily to our programs, but the adults required mentoring. I fault not change per se but an unstable foundation—in the culture, in families and in communities—for widespread insecurity among adults. Those leadership lessons influenced my corporate practice to this day and also brought lasting psychic rewards.

No Trust, No Innovations

Teams, corporations, and communities will surmount the next decade's alterations only by structuring high trust and empathy among members. As we journey from assembly line thinking to a twenty-first-century mentality of innovation, people of all ages will need to develop self-trusting attitudes and reliable social relations.

Our government now encourages mentoring on a national scale. Locating trustworthy volunteers becomes a critical task. What criteria are being used to determine mentors' optimism and reliability? How will we know if mentors seek personal fulfillment above the needs of their protégés? Without that heartfelt, productive stewardship, empathy between adults and youngsters is tentative at best. Elders who sympathize with the subjective safety needs of children frequently lack the stable center, lucidity, or perhaps even the sanity to provide that. For instance, without at least one faith-filled, selfless relationship, it's doubtful that a young child will gain the virtuous reference points to structure inner security. One compassionate, calmly focused adult per household may be all that's required to endow children with enduring strength. Let me share an example:

I grew up in an intelligent, refined household. However, it was emotionally disruptive. I learned (and liked) to keep my own counsel and didn't automatically trust those in authority. Serious illness, financial ups and downs, and constant world travel contributed to early insecurities. My father died when I was thirteen and, before and after that, my mother spent years in one hospital after another. Decidedly, I drew character strength from my parents' moral excellence and kindness, but my grandmother was my stabilizer. Unobtrusively, she'd watch over us, available if needed. Her constancy counterbalanced the chaos. To ground myself after my father died, I left the family fold for boarding school—never to return. The premature departure forced a premature independence, and school structures provided blessed routines and stability. It wasn't an ideal setup, but it apparently armed me with a decent enough foundation for a productive life. Not hardship but self-doubt—fear of living—cripples us. Consequently, my definition of trust has always included *self*-trust: confidence in one's own ability to face and master trouble. That mastery is rooted in the development of a creative, spiritual reflex that strengthens with use, as we solve problems or pit ourselves against seeming adversity. And when I use the term "self-trust," of course I mean the deep, intuitive knowing that the prophet Isaiah detailed: "Thine ears shall hear a word behind thee, saying, 'This is the way, walk ye in it.' "[1]

CONGRUENCY BUILDS TRUST

E was our person-centered guide to what I'd call the skills of congruency. She demonstrated empathy concretely, with her behavior. Slowly, we admitted that what we felt down deep was slippery—hard to express. To the extent that we put ourselves in others' shoes and attended to and understood their feelings, they felt better and moved beyond those feelings. We did, too. As we courageously revealed who we were, we grew. Our staff's sympathetic responses multiplied. Instead of resisting solutions, as a group we trusted our move toward them.

The progression toward healing choices resides at the heart of person-centered psychology. Healing choices are the soul of both sound mental health and spiritual wholeness.[2] Contemporary conflict-resolution methods use these exact principles as a veritable tonic for troubled human relations of all sorts. Largely by example, E taught us how to hear others nonviolently, how to listen to the *feelings* underneath someone's remarks rather than reacting for or against the *content* of the message.

The more we adults listened with our entire being to what a youngster felt, the more that child felt accepted and flourished. If we heard others' feelings without criticizing their remarks, somehow they heard their own truths. Over time, we learned to do what E so capably clarified, and our less judgmental stance established a protocol of emotional protection for nearly everyone: staff, parents, and students.

Bit by bit, we felt safer with one another. When angry, we found words to express that. We didn't pretend to be cheerful or loving when feeling otherwise. Nor did we hide our vulnerabilities by smartly fending off barbs as if we didn't care. When someone was unkind to us, we said, "Ouch. That hurts." This too extended collective genuineness. Of course, not everyone opened up at this level. A few people feigned contentment, and the disgruntled continued to buzz complainingly behind the scenes. However, the majority of us disclosed our joys and hurts without inordinate drama, entering into that authentic dialogue that nurtures trust and ingenuity. In that spirit of oneness, we built a productive environment.

Soon we adults were becoming down-to-earth in our defenses, as tender and as idiosyncratic as any child. Shy people protected themselves in one way, extroverts in another. We learned the truth of the poet Rilke's notion that humans strive to remain uniquely themselves at all costs. In the midst of a bustling, conventional school, growth flourished. I've repeatedly witnessed the exact outcome in every corporate setting whose managers possess the mentor's spirit. Imagine the whole-scale uplift that might result if governments and, say, the health care industry were mentored by high-trust, empathic influencers.

Philosopher Eli Siegel proposed that feeling *safe* in the world is the greatest instinct of our unconscious.[3] E contributed enormously to our subjective safety, convincing me that trust can be learned on a grand scale. That was also a viable, lasting gift to children: If adults are relaxed and trusting, young people thrive. I looked forward to E's day with us when we shared a cup of coffee and discussed all manner of things. Those talks cemented a friendship that lessened the loneliness of leadership.

MODELS OF TRUST AND WHOLENESS

We need not mourn the lack of productive mentors: The mentor's *spirit* permeates all of life. Stories, even movies, are instructive and full of liberating potential. A film need not be extraordinary in its technical, artistic, or conceptual presentation to exert a mentoring influence. Our usual mind, programmed as it is by culture and the context of existence, tends to fix on what's visible. Normally, we attach ourselves to people, to places, to creative projects or things. Attachments stupefy, render us helpless. Perhaps we're wrapped up in limiting illusory beliefs, muddled about our potential, or still at the affect of childish feelings and dependencies. To widen our scope, movies need only tell stories that give us glimpses—however fanciful—of our obsessions or difficulties or bring us hope.

Stories of hope enlarge us, resolve fears, and restore us as particular, distinctive individuals with as yet unrealized dreams. Not just stories, but deep awareness—as in prayer—can activate our power to choose goodness, vitality, and love. Saint Paul called these higher experiential openings (and I paraphrase,) "the eyes of our heart" and said prayer lets us know what is the hope of God's calling for us.

Many people seem to prefer safety to that knowing. They shun spiritual awareness. Watching films alertly lets us inch toward our truths in relative comfort. In the privacy of our rooms, we spot heroisms and self-deception, perhaps remembering who we are—at best.

Movies are often simple parables that retell spiritual myths. As Jung wrote, myths are not precisely fiction but rather deep, abiding truths about reality that humankind longs to have affirmed repeatedly. In these pages I suggest that movies are psychically productive even when they're obvious, elementary fairy tales. An uncomplicated story—like *Babe* or *The Shawshank Redemption,* can reinforce tough truths, teach us to endure, or apply ourselves fruitfully. *All* fine art conveys the mentor's spirit by encouraging honest self-examination.

A GENTLE EXPLORATION OF TRUST

Selected movies can portray trust, congruency, and other elevated attributes of being. In *To Kill a Mockingbird,* small-town lawyer Atticus Finch (Gregory Peck) assumes the defense of a black man accused of raping a white woman. The self-possessed lawyer, a philosopher type, is a widower living with his children in a Depression-era southern town. Atticus Finch accepts the unpopular case despite sensing that a vengeful community and lynch mob could harm him, his two children, and his client. Adapted from author Harper Lee's classic novel, the movie provides a model of the self-actualizing temperament. Atticus Finch shares many traits with other self-actualizing adults, among which are

- a superior perception of reality
- an increased acceptance of self, others, and nature
- increased spontaneity and solution orientation (as opposed to being problem centered)
- increased detachment and autonomy (greater resistance to enculturation, the opinions of others, etc.)
- democratic character structure (including improved interpersonal relationships and increased identifications with the human species)[4]

Finch radiates trustworthiness, and that is the point here. If you review the movie, give thought to keeping a journal to jot down your reactions or, as English teachers have suggested to me, discussing with a study group your answers to inquiries like the following:

- In your eyes, what elements of wholeness (e.g., body language, nonverbal cues) does Finch (or any of the other characters) embody?
- How does the film restore your memories of your *own* diverse, loving aims and sensibilities?

- How did your parents' influences and examples shape your current ability to endure difficulty, move beyond fear, or trust others?
- What are some *other movies* that might contribute significant stories, characters, and images of hope, compassion, or encouragement?[5]

TRUSTWORTHY MENTORS HELP US MOVE ON

For several years, I'd felt a desire to leave the public sector. My administrative activities felt restrictive, and I wanted to break out of that mold, not merely change it. I knew that affirming those vocational truths would force me to alter work, friendships, and an overall way of life. It would invite inevitable agony—profound loss, separations, grief—and carry me over a threshold of material security I believed I sorely needed. There was no way to rush a passage that demanded more courage (and self-trust) than I then had. Those higher-order virtues arrived at a snail's pace, accompanying the incremental refinement of values, character, and goals that the transition itself demanded. I kept my plans to myself, except in the most general way, living with years of ambiguity. Leadership pundit John W. Gardner has proposed that one learns to tolerate as one's norm the multiple concerns layered within these ambiguous transitions. Forging an authentic, unbounded life seems to be a *process,* not an event.

Productive mentors solve routine problems innovatively by maintaining a certain detachment about them. It's an art worth cultivating. As Gardner writes, when engulfed by unresolved questions we need "high tolerance for internal conflict, a willingness to suspend judgment,"[6] before achieving a degree of comfort. In other words, self-trust helps us sustain the tension of *not* knowing what our future holds. While pondering such matters, I'd converse with E about other, work-related worries. Rarely a silent sufferer, I gratefully unloaded those cares on E. Somehow her "be as you are" philosophy helped me choose growth over comfort. E never sermonized, "You *should* do thus or such." She just reminded me of previous successes, listened with empathy, and somehow the inner cues suggested, "This is the way, walk ye in it."

The mentor's spirit furthers all-out living. A year before resigning to start my firm, I revealed my intentions to E. She probably anticipated that decision, didn't blink an eye and simply said, "Your future is calling. It's time you left this cozy nest."

The 4th Lesson

PRODUCTIVITY IS CONTAGIOUS

———◆◦❈◦◆———

The love behind authentic, effortless giving frees up our life, lets us unfold to be more of ourselves. This is simply productive: The more genuine we are, the more good we have to give.

THROUGHOUT THEIR LIVES, productive individuals grow increasingly authentic. You might say they relax into who they are and realize their creative powers without the phoniness so common to some others. Hypocrisy is abhorrent to the productive type who "is *related, transcendent, rooted;* and he has a strong sense of *identity* with a stable *frame of orientation* toward his life."[1]

Healthy mentoring flows from productive types because, as we have seen, loving life they encourage life in others. This is key, so I repeat it. When our relationships are mutually liberating, we connect to people without artificiality. By contrast, unhealthy mentors try to fool or exploit us. Their words seem to deprive us of dignity or safety, and somehow that robs us of vitality. They may be ultra-aggressive or manipulative. They may not hear or respect our disclosures, could thwart our wishes, and generally don't—perhaps can't—guide us to true liberty. Erich Fromm's description of "productiveness" influenced my ideas about healthy mentoring, and I share Fromm's and Maslow's view that when self-actualizing growth is blocked, life-denying impulses increase. Fromm's term for the opposite of the productive type is *necrophilous*. The word means "lover of death and decay," a cancerous life orientation, the "quintessence of evil." Epitomized by ultra-authoritarian repression, necrophilous types ran rampant under Nazi rule where control of others, detached annihilation (or torture) of life, and militaristic rituals were celebrated. While most of us have mixtures of productive and unproductive responses, we observe in extreme nonproductive types an absorption with dead systems and an unsettling "concern with mechanical, nonhuman gadgetry." As Fromm explains: "The necrophile who is interested in photography takes pictures of people, but his interest is directed to the quality and sophistication of his *camera;* he listens to music, but his love is for experimentation with his complicated stereophonic receiver; he loves time-saving appliances, but even the simplest addition is done on a calculator; even the shortest walk to a grocery store is reason to drive there by car. In effect the necrophilous character substitutes an affinity for *technique* and for *technology* in place of the [productive] person's affinity for life, for people, beauty."[2]

Productive mentors are spontaneously gifted *life* artists. As parents, they'll devote their lives to their offspring, yet won't pamper to excess. They'll raise responsible, self-reliant individuals who in turn contribute to life. As teachers, they'll love the truth and beauty of their topics, want only good for pupils, and weave their passions into every hour of every effort, thereby awakening awe and love of learning in others and *earning* their students' trust. (Those who enter the profession for a secure paycheck lack such fire. Consequently they impart little of value and receive precious little in return.) Every teacher with such positivity is fulfilled by the reciprocal love and trust arising from student and community relationships. Teachers who serve their pupils' authenticities experience a magical, life-affirming vocation.

A Personal Story

Despite a hunger for greater challenge, saying good-bye to a close community of colleagues generated a piercing grief. In 1980, when I left the sanctuary of public education for the unsheltered realities of my human resource practice, here's what I felt: I loved teaching. The principalship was, to me, a leadership challenge of considerable merit and a natural extension of my classroom's reach, a vehicle to add value to children and learning within the context of a broader community. The intellectual stimulation of those leadership tasks—adult teamwork and large-scale, complex communication projects—intensified my love of learning.

Only when I felt larger and more competent than the responsibilities I'd been assigned could I leave teaching. For me, this was one of those spontaneous sailings when one simply *knows* it's time to ship out. Agonizing or not, one just shoves off. In many ways, my educational associates were like a second family. I'd suffered so many hurts in childhood. Why was I imposing new distress on myself? For me, leaving was a painful self-surgery that demanded all my resolve. I made false starts. Each attempt laid bare those childhood wounds: countless good-byes, countless seeming privations. Each old trauma required healing, a mending process that took years (and even therapy) to reconcile what had become a conscious mourning for losses sustained in early life.

When sufficiently regenerated, I resigned, ready to ride the current of my life or, paraphrasing Shakespeare, risk losing all its promise.

Pulling up that anchor meant overhauling my original goals as an educator. That took months. Then came the whirlwind of starting up a thrilling venture (my own enterprise, after all). The process completely absorbed my attention. And a quick success left little time to integrate the departure or reflect on how much I'd loved, and now missed, my students. True, I respected and even needed my new corporate associates. How incredibly refreshing to work with adventuresome, entrepreneurial adults. Still, service to all ages of children had absolutely enhanced my life.

The sum total of my professional existence to that point had been regenerated by relationships with youngsters. Perhaps I chose to work with children because I'd lost my own childhood. In a substantive sense, the young had mentored me. To teach effectively, I had to *function* in relationship: become sensitive to the instinctive playfulness of youth, accommodate the innocence and irresistible zest of students. I'd become productive—had to consider what children needed, how they felt, what I might do to enhance their growth. An inescapable restoration of character followed mutual regard. It always does. A teacher is helpful only when she, too, is learning, guiding, and intuitively empathizing with all students (not just the agreeable or obedient ones), searching out their talents and temperaments for hidden potential, and loving each one impersonally enough to let that child move on independently when it comes time. (Smothering is the kiss of death of the mentor's spirit and always hints of fear and overcontrol.) These are critical skills for anyone who works with others as an executive or as a helping professional.

LOVE IS PURE BEING

The youngsters I'd encountered in my classroom, and later as a principal, were the living, breathing reason for having entered education in the first place. Always totally real, children had taught me that in giving *we* receive; in giving we are made most joyful—fearless, really. Furthermore, the love behind authentic, effortless giving frees us, lets us unfold to be more of ourselves. This is simply productive: The more genuine we *are,* the more good we have to give, for in genuineness is love.

In using the word "love," I do not mean sentimental or romantic feelings. Nor do I refer to familial love, the blood ties that bind. Love may be a feeling of affection. It may not. Love may bond us to our birth family. It may not. Love is always what we *are,* the foundational energy and life-force of pure being. At all times, love challenges us to respond to others, to the littlest details and to the invisible substrata of daily life—from itself, the core of what we are. Who among us has perfected that sort of giving? Yet that love alone is productive, requires us to remain aware, alert to what needs doing, and to forget ourselves while yielding ourselves *to* love.

Our conscious, surface worry could be that we're not being loved. Fromm proposes that, deeper still, we worry *that we are not loving.* Perhaps he means that we fear that by not loving we do not truly come to life. The mentor's spirit in children calls us to our living by provoking us to act with selfless caring: "The ability to love depends on one's capacity to emerge from narcissism, and from the incestuous fixation to mother and clan; it depends on our capacity to grow, to develop a productive orientation in our relationship toward the world and ourselves.

This process of emergence, of birth, of waking up, requires one quality as a necessary condition: *faith.* The practice of the art of loving requires the practice of faith."[3]

YOUTH POSSESSES THE MENTOR'S SPIRIT

It's said that a teacher's first class is the one he or she remembers throughout life. I'd add only that the memory of my first classes lingers because they reflected a part of myself I'd hidden. Those children weren't individual mentors, but as a generic energy the classes conveyed the mentor's spirit. Something spiritual—trust, spontaneity, enjoyment of the moment, love of learning—amplified those traits in me. This relates to earlier remarks about projection: We meet ourselves coming and going, in whomever we admire (or dislike). In his book on leadership, Garry Wills suggests that if you tell him who your favorite leaders are, he'll show you who you are.[4] The same rule applies to mentors: You show me your mentors, I'll show you who *you* are. As we search for our mentors, let's remember that youth possesses that spirit, too. Productive attributes are ageless. It's a myth that only elders can guide.

Children convinced me that each of us gives to the other what we can, and idiosyncratically. That primal reflex of generosity tends to reflect vocation. Each not only gives distinctively, but also is most magnanimous to a discrete *set of others.* For instance, Picasso gave to others through his art; Einstein through his science; Julian of Norwich, the saintly anchorite, blessed others through her prayerful, solitary silence and subsequent written revelations. Some of my corporate colleagues give indefatigably to their workplace.

We give what we can, what we're born to give. In 1987, while writing the introduction to *Elegant Choices, Healing Choices,* I acknowledged some of this and wept, out of sheer gratitude, for the selfless generosity of the young. Their gladness and productivity was contagious—as somewhere I've heard it said, a "labor that tendeth to life."

PART II

———◆———

SILENCE INVITES
THE MENTOR'S
SPIRIT

The 5th Lesson

TRANSCENDENCE BOOSTS LEARNING

———◆◆◆———

When we're teaching ourselves what we need to know, we enter a transcendent zone that dissolves supposed problems. In pure realms of consciousness, no obstructions exist. I insist that transcendent learning and optimal growth are two sides of one coin.

IT'S SAID THAT success must be in *us* before it can be in our enterprise. Without infusing our subjective vitality into whatever we do, even our physical activity remains impotent. In line with this reasoning, whenever someone asks me how to insure a dynamic success, I answer: Learn to love silence, the sort that flows from a mind that's perfectly still. Interior stillness promotes the wisdom that penetrates experience with meaning and fulfillment. "Know thyself" and "Be thyself" are educative phrases as well as mentoring *and* developmental precepts. These edicts are rooted in silent realities, the "still, small voice." It takes focus, intent, and silence to know and to be ourselves.

Inward listening, approached patiently, fills us with the light of insight. Intelligent awareness, watchfulness, strengthens our influence skills or knack of reaching for relevant goals because as we "hear" our still, small voice, we sense our way toward outer effectiveness and apply our understandings to the affairs of daily life. There are numerous routes to such effectiveness.

Beauty, for one, draws us into silence, *"the* profound medium for spiritual growth."[1] Music (from birdsong to Bach) leads us inwardly. The theater, poetry, and dance can, too. Nobel Prize–winner Alexander Solzhenitsyn wrote that art might somehow save our world given beauty's tendency to transmit, if only briefly, "revelations unattainable by reason."[2]

In utter stillness most people grow self-aware. Shutting out intrusions from radio, television, or social chatter may at first trigger anxiety. What shall we do with our time? With practice, stillness delivers a sense of harmony, forgiveness, or oceanic love. Thoughts quiet down. We enter an unbounded state. Philosopher Max Picard wrote that silence and pure being are linked. That may explain why "inventors, scholars, artists and naturalists all value silence for their creative discoveries and personal renewal. . . . Children spontaneously stop their play to gaze up at the night sky. Instinctively, wordlessly, they are deepened, opened-up in some way by the sky's unfathomable, dynamic quiet. Without being told, they sense an imponderable void both within and without."[3]

Silence is not for everyone. However, silence is linked to learning. That fact can be universally appreciated. Serious study leads us inward, toward some degree of interior calm. To operate our various functions of mind, we must concentrate just so: look for the right fact, discard an irrelevancy, listen intently to a lecture. The studying habit of mind is but a prelude to the deep silence of, say, meditation, when true being controls scattered thoughts, stops the attention from darting about here and there. Managing the attention evokes serenity, internal calm. All meditation—indeed, learning as well—involves a managed attention. Whether enjoying a sunset, a candle flame, or a line of Scripture, we're moved beyond inattention into stillness. That mental "moving beyond" is a transcendence that brings insight and the revelations of vision.

To achieve twenty-first-century success, all of us (organizations, too) will first become successful *inwardly*. Progressive companies must sense this. They emphasize (and also sponsor) independent learning. These firms are merging the tenets of education, business, and spiritual growth and teem with lively thinkers who love their unique process of creative discovery. Whoever finds ways (and is encouraged) to teach themselves whatever they need to know eventually leverages their existing knowledge into novel, broader solutions. All such exploration benefits the greater good.

If either an individual or organization learns to *love* learning, the fear of change or the so-called mistake evaporates. When we're teaching ourselves what we need to know, we enter a transcendent zone that dissolves supposed problems. In pure realms of consciousness, no obstructions exist. This is why I insist that transcendent learning and optimal growth are two sides of one coin—love in action—found in stillness.

A PERSONAL STORY

Years of corporate activity and writing more than a dozen business articles and several books preceded my ability to articulate an incipient framework about transcendent learning. I was teaching myself what *I* longed to know: What does it take to be optimally creative and spiritually self-actualizing? Along the road to discovery, timeless truths surfaced: that wholeness requires an active, unbounded learning; that creative adults make consciously self-disciplining choices; that quick fixes, passive therapies, or dominating, directive authority figures rarely enhance resourcefulness. My driving bias was that, ideally, educative models would raise self-awareness, and that resulted in a three-cornered prototype for a transcendent learning program:

- authentic dialogue with a trusted other
- self-initiated study (of any intensely absorbing theme)
- the management of attention (mainly through consciously improved choices in low-risk areas)

Slowly, that evolved into the Positive Structuring method, about which I'll say more shortly.[4] Merely engaging in substantial conversations about such prospects prompted some individuals to choose healthy growth.

At first, I simply immersed myself in the relevant issues of my own life—corporate leadership being one. Learning patterns I'd spotted in primary children, in teachers, and in graduate students reemerged vividly in the corporate setting. These patterns nudged me to test my ideas about transcendent learning on stable, gifted managers who enjoyed abstractions, attended inwardly with ease, and playfully translated abstract insight into practical, operating effects. Effective employees—those who got along with others, who solved problems independently and with sound judgment—were highly intuitive. They trusted the still, small voice within.

All educators have their areas of keen interest. Some are incredibly patient with remedial learners. Others love multimedia work. My specialty entailed designing models and learning climates that promote talent and robust creativity. This explains why my clients tend to be inspired entrepreneurs, business artists.

Early on, my corporate practice evolved into an educational service that sparked innovation and self-directed growth.

Having always presumed that healthy adults could uncover their truths, it seemed they could teach themselves how to learn about their optimal growth. Education draws us out—to the world, to others, to a practical livelihood. It also draws us in—to the depths of ourselves. In essence, learning leads us *to* ourselves. Ideally, leadership development comes under that same broad philosophical umbrella of learning. By protecting the superordinate goals of each person, leadership development shares education's lofty purpose of drawing out nobility of effort and functional contribution despite the drudgery of life.

FASCINATIONS HOLD THE MENTOR'S SPIRIT

In retrospect, it seems I was designing programs and processes that, had they been available, would have mentored me. This is why I emphasize for the despairing who crave in-person mentors, that the mentor's *spirit* is sufficiently transforming. For example, I noticed that some unseen love moves my clients toward a distinctive unfolding of their life's plan. Even chance remarks can trigger that movement. Here's one illustration:

No family member guided me toward college. Conditions were far too disruptive in my childhood for such responsible nurturing. I can honestly report that I took myself to college. Determined to earn a degree, I paid my own way and figured out where I was headed. The opinion of one caring English teacher and one stewardly principal reinforced my thinking. Glistening with pride over some test score, those two insisted I was college material.

Frankly, I thought I was too, despite a kind of primary process (or creative) thinking that made it nearly impossible to follow linear directions. Their words bolstered my watery courage.

Later, as a self-supporting undergraduate toiling at minimum wage jobs, I nearly flunked out of college for want of regular meals and sleep. It was a wretched existence. All I did was work. I was perennially exhausted and scared and hungry. In that order. My fiancé would bring me chicken sandwiches on luscious homemade bread after his mother heard that I routinely fainted in the library from lack of food. She'd stack as many sandwiches as she could load into a brown paper sack, along with heaps of freshly baked strudel. I've never forgotten her generosity. Proper study habits and graduate school were the farthest things from my mind. And anyway, I didn't have the grades to be accepted.

One day while handing back an essay, a professor said, "Study skills aside, if you don't earn your Ph.D., you'll be throwing away your life." His offhanded counsel grabbed my attention. Something within heard a ring of truth, and I consciously chose to listen. That casual comment from a virtual stranger (the man hardly spoke to me again) nudged me another step closer to my compelling purposes.

As it turns out, my work itself, flowing as it has out of the tides of inner meanings and peak experiences, became a luxurious self-educative dance, a true vocation. Vocation is one vehicle for boundless growth, a means of imparting value to ourselves and others through what we feel are sacred tasks or archetypical images (long held in mind). My most sumptuous options revealed themselves only *after* I left the public sector for what C. S. Lewis calls the "utter east." At my World's End is a religious reality made all the richer by a contemplative existence.

Previously I'd suppressed restlessness, convinced that my true interests didn't matter. Ultimately, to succeed on my terms, I had to listen inwardly, embrace my quirks and differences, and learn to honor a creative disposition. Artist Ben Shahn described that temperament—one that characterizes artists—as "impatience, unwillingness to be led, fear of being trapped in stable situations—[even] an arrogant belief in one's own authority . . . an intense boredom with propriety and all its triteness."[5] Reading Shahn I felt understood at last. That same relief hit me when reading Thomas Merton and Evelyn Underhill, which shows how the mentor's spirit works.

In the corporate sector, everywhere I looked I saw talented men and women discounting their truths and finest tendencies while honoring a self-demeaning unreality. Smart, idealistic adults seemed hampered by the same subjective constraints that I'd let block me. Too many otherwise gifted adults appeared constricted. Hesitation, misdirected ambition, an inability or reticence to accept their own daring forbid their saying, "This freedom, that love, that occupation is what I want."

My rapport was instant with clients who glimpsed the possibility of a vocation. For one thing, we fully encountered each other, were somehow kindred spirits. In our discussions, we divulged what we wanted. My new corporate role was wonderfully multifaceted. Even as a novice, I functioned as strategist and coach, was trusted as a confidant and peacemaker. All that without benefit of titles or position power. How refreshing.

Progressively impertinent choices delivered fresh reservoirs of energy and an audacity that felt intimidating at first. With heightened commitment to our vocational pursuits comes a willingness to be distinctive, to stand alone, to be known. So comes the probability of rejection. Our confidence or inventiveness may alienate others, but this effect is more than offset by the fulfillment, goodwill, and love of service that emanates from a genuine vocation. (I don't know a single person engaged with a vocation who'd give it up for anything else.) Service to others taught me to take prudent risks and try out new leadership skills and tolerate discomfort. Instead of squandering energy on what I feared might happen, progressively I invested my inventive forces in each goal. This is simply efficient.

Rather than dwell on the predicament, I embodied bits of my solutions in low-risk prototypes as artfully as possible. That practice revealed larger bits of the solution. First by explaining that method, then by writing about it,[6] I shared the model with others while noticing a transcendent learning taking place. These coaching sessions seemed to guide executives' thought processes through educative explanations, yet left enough room for them to play around with aggregates of their solution—independently. In other words, without me.

Our mentoring heart awakens with maturity. First comes truth telling and sufficient self-respect to risk being real. It follows that we'll appreciate life enough to want and trust others' success—to wish them well as they set sail for the depths of their unknowns. Those trustful attitudes can't be feigned. Moreover, there's a developmental logic to that certitude: If our mentors trust us with their truths and well wishes, we become animated by what St. John of the Cross called "a seed of fire": "very minute, burning and full of power . . . like a vast fire of love and [the soul sees] that the point of its virtue is in the heart of the spirit."[7]

PRODUCTIVE MENTORS LEARN BY DOING

Insights come not just through transcendent experiences but continually, through honest talks with trusted colleagues as we consider conflicts or a setback. Leadership development requires in-depth, individualized dialogue about applying the basics to everyday decision making. Many able leaders, lacking intimate trusting relationships, use Scripture's parables or a wilderness outing with virtual strangers to stimulate their inner mentor. Any activity that restores us or arouses our productive tendencies seems fruitful.

One of the first executives I worked with in an informal, relational context was CH, a manager with unusual breadth and depth of understanding of her corporate function. CH was a new human resource director in a huge multinational corporation. We'd met a year earlier at a conference and realized, within moments of our first conversation, that we shared a similar excitement about transformational leadership.

During our several years of working together, I grew to value CH's friendship. In private sessions, I felt comfortable enough to blurt out my latest ideas. Eager to mesh theory with routine business, I must have babbled incoherently. Good-natured soul that she is, CH greeted those ramblings with levelheadedness. Little did she know that by listening, she coaxed from me a seminal, educative method.

Many personnel professionals view themselves as custodians of the corporate handbook. They're Policy Police, controlling and micromanaging others with rules. They interpret policies rigidly and consequently box in and reign over their constituents with nitpicky regulations. Largely incapable of flexible collaboration, such individuals constrict profitable innovation. I've worked with human resource professionals who behave as if their company was a social service agency. These enablers are dedicated to "curing" performance deficits through endless counseling sessions. Some just like to hear themselves talk, but the worst offenders actually *rewrite* policy in a pathetic attempt to cover every conceivable managerial weakness with a rule. By comparison, CH called a problem what it was, then solved it pragmatically and with empathy.

CH is persuasive, a no-nonsense person. She's also funny. Our days were unbelievably chaotic, yet we had an outrageously fine time. Many late afternoons found us lazing about in CH's office, jovially managing stress by stuffing ourselves with M&Ms and ice cream, chortling about the bizarre nature of our task. After exhausting our available stash of bonbons, we'd call it a day—and go out for Szechuan food.

We were facilitating a massive and complex corporate restructuring, bracing up vast numbers of angry, frightened workers and assuring them the sky was not falling. How futile to try to convince a work team to remain serene and lucid within that fluctuating environment. One had to *demonstrate* calm, exhibit objectivity, actually *be* clear minded. Every workshop, focus group, and development session had to *illustrate* the ideas and processes we were proposing. Easier said than done. We watched seasoned senior managers disseminate good news about benefits or raises. In their unsettled state they made their work group more anxious. Employees left these "good news" meetings in tears or with migraines. When CH passed along a positive dispatch, people heard her and felt better. That pattern proved that in times of crisis effective leaders must speak not only to our intellect but also to the heart—from their own heart. If they don't trust what they're say-ing, neither will we.

Leadership development travels the same winding path as creative problem solving. There are seeming stalls, growth spurts and periods of bewilderment. In fact, during these delays, a sort of hardiness is growing—resilience, the lessening of bondage to circumstances, the maturity of an inner dynamic. Perhaps our mentors will coax out good ideas by asking us to speak plainly about them. Or they'll wait unobtrusively to watch what tran-spires without their intervention. That sort of development is gradual and allows our understanding of our own infinite versa-tility to unfold. We can cope; we can move on. Many executives, however, require instant outcomes. They can't stand the frustra-tion of the apparent stalls of growth. If conversation lags, if there's no immediate closure, if there's unresolved dissent, they get im-patient, irritated, even a little nutty. CH is one of those uncom-mon individuals with a healthy tolerance for circuitous learning and has raised her own leadership sights. She demonstrated her multiple talents variously: in corporate meetings as a leader; in graduate school as a student; in her juggler's capacity as parent, spouse, and employee; and over the years by unveiling her own vision of a meaningful future. Today CH mentors other mentors. She's what I'd call a transcendent learner (although I doubt she'd ever call herself that).

Transcendent learning involves that rightly focused mind that lifts us, perceptually, above anxieties or yokes that bind. Here's where our answers live. That mind looks up, out, and over cir-cumstances. Never back.

The 6th Lesson

AUTHENTIC DIALOGUE
MATURES LEADERS

———◆━❋━◆———

Authentic dialogue promotes mature self-governing work teams who "walk the talk."

W E EMPOWER OTHERS through our wholeness. It takes a humane, spiritually mature mentor at every level of an organization or family to draw out that completeness. Inner stillness is part of that extraction and sustains the mentor's spirit.

We must be watchful and firmly grounded to hear the humanity and intimate guidance within ourselves. As Scripture puts it, the Spirit of truth abides within our stillness and that's our teacher. Hasidic philosopher Martin Buber wrote that *only* in stillness does our soul burst through the commotion of everyday life. Stillness resides at our inmost core, in the sacred silence between our thoughts and plans. Most of the time, we talk too much—a dualistic, good/bad chatter that often produces counterproductive results and betrays our hostilities in the process, as even the Psalmist realized:

> . . . The words of his mouth were smoother than butter,
>> but war was in his heart:
>> his words were softer than oil,
>> yet were they drawn swords[1]

75

Stillness of being untangles us. Every ancient culture appears to venerate the simplified life, the pure awareness or innocence of being that unlocks promise. Each of us knows that state. A stroll at the seashore puts things into perspective whenever it cultures inner silence. A tranquil friend comforts us by lessening our confusion. The sound of rain pattering on a gravel path calms us.

Some individuals seem poorly equipped to tolerate much silence. For example, psychotic or borderline types (or the emotionally immature) shouldn't attempt to court silence through meditation or yogic techniques. In a way, as our most profound level of existence, inner silence courts *us*. Furthermore, no one can seize stillness like a Big Mac at a drive-through window or coax it out with emotional theatrics. Silence simply is. It reinforces being, the first mentoring key discussed. It spawns an inner dialogue. Through its integrating peace, without fuss, we work out the puzzles of existence:

- What brings me to life?
- What's worth doing?
- What deep meanings fuel my enthusiasms?
- What (or who) drains my energy and optimism?
- What (or who) renews my hope, drive, and vision of possibilities?
- What does destiny or "doing God's will" mean to me at this stage of life?
- What might I do—what *must* I do—to honor the life I've been given?

One need not make a big to-do of such inquiries. In and through silence, insights remind us of unfinished business. The most mundane activities—square dancing, sudsing the dinner dishes, listening to Mozart or Prince—can lead us inward to stillness where answers exist.

The greatest leaders understand these links between silence, self-renewal, and active tasks like weeding a garden. Leaders of merit play golf or the banjo for creative renewal and rarely squander time, energy, or emotions. They order their daily schedule so as to gain the poise under pressure so essential to their job and decision making. Without that balance, even conversation becomes scattered and superficial. It's not surprising that inner stillness promotes healthy, two-way exchanges. Fragmented individuals set up obstacles to conversation. A nervous tic, a drifting attention gives them an out. Given their symptoms, they need not relate.

Authentic Dialogue Lets Us "Walk the Talk"

Some individuals can't make a logical link between everyday decisions and a company value like "We strive for excellence" or "We care about people." Clueless as to what those values entail, they wonder how, practically, to "strive for excellence" or "care about people."

Picture, if you can, how it might feel to explore such behavioral subtleties during relaxed discussions at weekend retreats or after a staff meeting. Imagine being asked to observe and bring with you to these sessions actual case histories that tangibly depict the issues under examination. Properly facilitated, informal two-way discussions convert theory into nuts-and-bolts relevance. Sometimes an inspired follow-through results from that understanding. (Not *always*.) Abstractions like "caring for people" become concrete realities when managers feel secure (and are adroit) enough to field questions from the floor about the nuances of ideas like excellence and caring, especially when group members take responsibility for enlivening the conversation. This is dialogue: *mutually animating discourse.*

Corporate recruitment polls indicate that relationship skills are among the top-rated, most desirable qualities for new hires. In our supposedly enlightened industrial climate, it's still the rare manager who possesses a temperament for "mutually animating discourse." Some corporations reward supervisors for caring more for project turnaround time, numbers or P&L ratios than people. Others hire robotic types who believe people get in the way of tasks.

Cardboard communicators are rigid and devitalized. Their demeanor lulls us into a stupor. In business settings, they're the folks who present ideas in hackneyed terms or read their agenda items directly from a memo. At staff meetings, some speakers turn off the lights, turn on the technology, and, with pointer in hand, address close associates from the shadows of the room, forcing their listeners to squint at computer-generated symbols on a screen in the dark.

The best-run companies routinely set aside nonstructured time for *exchanging* ideas. These dialogue sessions are a microcosm of corporate life: You get out what you put into it. From breakfast meetings to focus groups to after-work assemblies with an entire company, informal forums can develop (and train) executives in the art of dialogue, help them "sell an idea," or practice active listening and other interpersonal skills. Structured meetings continue as their norm, but department heads and corporate leaders talk *with* people as a matter of course and corporate culture. By being available and real, these managers pump life into relationships and shared values. Their way of *being,* not clichéd phrases, helps a team grasp where the company is going, why it's headed there, what it hopes to accomplish, and why the founder and senior team's expectations are as they are. With the give-and-take of these exchanges, a work group easily envisions its role. The team's words or choices can then reflect a broad comprehension of the corporate vantage point. In a real sense, authentic dialogue promotes mature, *self*-governing work teams who "walk the talk." That mature self-governance is a spiritual faculty culled in the silent, deep heart of wisdom's still, small voice.

In his book on leadership, Max DePree states that an essential intimacy of leadership "arises from, and gives rise to, strong relationships. Intimacy is one way of describing the relationship we all desire with work."[2] DePree suggests that we grow by living with our questions (not by knowing all the answers). His point so rightly reinforces the rule that authentic dialogue, by airing various points of view, promotes a sense of oneness with others, as we learn to hear them.

Senior managers may find it helpful to hold quarterly dialogue meetings. As one participant repeatedly puts it, these are discussion—*not* decision-making—sessions. There's mutual agreement in advance about what will be discussed. Everyone comes to the table prepared to participate. Typically, I'll distribute books, articles, and audios and even show film clips to stimulate ideas. Once a group grows accustomed to receiving a rich assortment of preparatory material, enthusiasm skyrockets. Members take the initiative to distribute their favorite resource offerings when introducing topics they want to discuss. Their emotional availability—*being* with others—increasingly informs and motivates the group.

A Personal Story

Lacking financial independence or business connections, I built my corporate practice from scratch. Setting my own agenda I designed the firm's services to maximize creative freedom—mine and others. I declined projects with bureaucracies (for instance, government agencies or munitions firms) and shunned organizations requiring lengthy proposal bids for projects. Admittedly, such companies never beat down my door. I hungered to innovate freely, to research and write and, bent on exercising my leadership, wanted to work with like-minded associates.

A favorite associate once predicted I'd attract clients that matched my creative style. His forecast turned out to be accurate. The companies that retained my firm also recruited charismatic entrepreneurs, who in turn hired inventive, high-energy executives. We all craved meaningful freedom, not a do-anything license but creative autonomy in our area of expertise. We sought protection from what we called micromanaging control freaks who, with incremental subtlety, deny individual responsibility.

From the outset, my clients spoke of a wish for liberty: Young and old alike desired health, prosperity, the chance to experiment, and stimulating ideas and quick-witted associates—the blessings every cogent achiever wants. Talent, the impulse to contribute something rare and valuable, the wish for wholesome growth prodded us all. Surrounded by numerous birds of a similar (and, I thought, beautiful) feather, to this day, it's not clear who was guiding whom. I suppose this blurred line between the mentor and the protégé occurs because, as a friend pointed out, a kind of symbiotic relationship occurs between the two. Moreover, those with a mature mentor's spirit sense oneness everywhere and draw that rapport out of others, too.

Some executives reflect their humanity through each detail of their functioning. A man I'll call R was like that—one of an elite, relatively young crew of energized managers I met during my first long-term assignment. I'd been retained by R's senior management, an inspired bunch of entrepreneurs that included quite a few ex-military officers. This was my "dream team," a dream assignment, and R's elevated ideals reflected the mentality of those who ran the company. His empathy for the sensibilities of his corporate leadership soon propelled him into an upper circle of contributors.

Even as a fledgling consultant, I received carte blanche to show what I could do. What an awakening: How unlike my public sector experience when, despite a track record of proven successes, I'd had to downplay each new idea. With that first corporate client, no maneuvering was required. Provided leadership acumen and practical strides increased, I pretty much ran the program. A senior VP—a West Point graduate, I think—gave me that chance. Perched on the same philosophical wire, we clicked instantly. Over informal coffees and in small, formal groups, R and I and others compared management philosophies, exploring all variants of leadership theory and style. We simulated far-out, futuristic solutions and played forecasting games. Some of our scenarios turned out to be prophetic. We expressed enormous idealism about work and twenty-first-century, global relationships. It was a rarefied dialogue among associates who reveled in their own competence. (At the time, one colleague's motto was, "Precision is the only standard.") We considered our efforts worthwhile and relished that improvisational environment. As a client said, "It's a *post*-graduate school: I'm paid big bucks to learn as much as possible about what interests me most." Once again, I had the impression that effectual teams are ensemble players. Whether executing a business plan or a baroque melody, precision comes when people are in tune, practiced in their art of synergy.

TRAITS OF MATURE CONTRIBUTORS: FIDELITY IN FLUX

Those informal talks led to more structured dialogue sessions: regular, if less rambling, exchanges about such ideals as integrity and what it means to invest oneself in a life's work. I had, by then, begun writing on these subjects and was eager to hear my clients' views. R seemed intuitively motivated to actualize his deepest purposes. Unlike some who chased promotions to pad their wallets or impress others (but who, once advanced, required constant spoon-feeding on the art of leadership), R grasped the big picture and the details of industry. He was developmentally ready for greater responsibility, a disposition observable in young students as well as adults and one having less to do with chronological age than with emotional set.

Despite technical expertise, not all managers are inwardly equipped—ready—to face the ambiguities of leadership. Executive development programs should provide multiple tiers of offerings. With fast-track clients in mind, I designed a complement of materials and programs for mature leaders and within two years had limited my practice to that group.

One knows when one is in the company of a seasoned colleague. These adults are prepared to grow. They encourage others' growth and possess several shared qualities of readiness:

- sound judgment
- independent thinking
- a tendency to think divergently
- good humor
- definite purpose
- moral elevation and reliability
- fidelity
- honorable interpersonal proclivities

R illustrates the trait of fidelity. Loyal to a cluster of enduring values, he is faithful to both family and spiritual realities. No corporate entity, not even one with power to remunerate him handsomely, ran his life. Psychiatrist Erik Erikson defined fidelity as our ability to sustain loyalties freely pledged while viewing the inevitable contradictions of our culture's value systems.[3] Leaders with mature fidelity don't follow orders mindlessly. For some a central stillness, for others constancy of faith, cultivates their ability to make responsible, value-based decisions. What textbooks now call "situational ethics"—a pragmatic, "what do circumstances require?" reflection—may follow, but never leads, fidelity.

Once R told me: "When all is said and done, ethical decisions are the best ones to make for shareholders and all concerned, including employees. In the final analysis, I've never been taken to task for an unpopular, but ethically based, decision."

THE LAW BEYOND THE LAW

Fidelity is a critical benchmark of leadership talent. Steadfastness makes it possible to grapple with the enigma of being fully human in imperfect settings. Leaders with obvious talent reconcile such paradox. I touched on this point in the last chapter. It may explain why some corporate heads, however gruff or inarticulate, excite us with their dreams, while others—more polished and superficially attractive—don't. The former highlight universally cherished aims (I've called this "speaking from the heart"). The latter wrap their statements in cerebral trappings that subtly undermine credibility. R's management style had character density or "is-ness." He'd lumber, not stride, down a hall. He'd think long and hard before answering your question. He kept confidences. The X factor behind that deliberate sphynx-like stance involved his deepest strata of being. Conversely, the shallow, snappy charisma that many executives and politicians project may energize us for a time, but rarely wears well.

CH and R seemed to make their existential choices from a spiritual base (and a moral foundation) that structured the creative elbowroom they enjoy today. I have heard that moral base called "the law beyond the law." When someone like R hears and obeys this law beyond the law, you notice his tangible stepping forth toward life. Amid the inadequacies or unfairness of living, you might feel inspired to follow suit. Truthful conversations with trusted companions introduce us to the law beyond the law. In corporate settings and other large organizations, the manipulative side of business—its covert networking and political machinations—can seem corrupt. The gifted, in particular, are acute injustice detectors. Others, observing the inconsistencies of corporate life, pretend not to notice.

The productive freedom we all require for spiritual or creative growth includes clear standards of conduct: self-discipline; honesty; a well-schooled, honorable conscience that reminds us of our noble goals. Some so deftly suppress their consciences that inner cues eventually grow fallow. In part, that's what it means to "have ears that do not hear and eyes that do not see." I sense that R attends to his internal radar about how to be true to himself within the context of family or community. This is another distinguishing feature of the mentor's spirit: It amplifies our internal voice, so that we hear others as we hear ourselves.

That inward listening is often inconvenient. One may become unbending. There are costs and consequences to being one's own. R adds, "Perhaps leadership is being the rebel in a go-along, get-along crowd. It may not be fun or popular to be a leader, but it can be self-fulfilling."

Loyalty to what we are—not to success per se—is fidelity's goal. Admitting our truths (limits as well as strengths), may necessitate changing jobs, relocating, or fulfilling some other actual need. We'll step out to new stages of genuineness, onto the vulnerable edge of our intuitive realities, and may feel a subjective imperative to do a thing before logically grasping *why* we must.

The inward listening habit ultimately involves our honest—perhaps sacrificial—response to what we've heard. I'm speculating that authentic growth demanded that R tread an arduous, perhaps lonely path: first to Asia, where he started up and developed the Japanese division of his corporation. After seven years, he was transferred back to America. As a seasoned manager he functions in a new cultural context with continually fluctuating teams of clients and associates.

I imagine that R now excels in cross-cultural human relations. His intrinsic gift is harmonizing Asian and Western value systems. It can't have been easy to relocate repeatedly with a wife and several young children. Had he stayed with his original firm, R might have avoided the turmoil of global dislocations—and also one of the grand adventures of his life.

The 7th Lesson

DEFINE TRUE SUCCESS

———◆◆◆◆———

Worldly (and whirlwind) success might have undone me had spiritual truth not revealed its attributes—such as beauty and harmony—as the unseen good behind any achievement I'd want.

A FAMOUS MASTER of meditation confounded her disciples when she spoke about the beauty of silence. "Silence holds truth, life's secrets—therefore it is beautiful." Her students grumbled: "But we've traveled miles and miles to hear *your* truths, your secrets, your inner beauty. How can we learn anything if you keep silent?" The guru replied, "Well, when I speak, you listen to the silence beneath my words." Still perplexed, they demanded more clarification: "*How* do we do that?" To which she replied, "After I finish talking, you shake everything I've said, as if shaking a tree, until only the truth remains. The truth that stays with you after my words drop away—*that's* beautiful, that comes from my silence, that's a beauty you can trust."[1] The beauty of that stillness taught me to use limits as a guide and to define the word *success* for myself.

Pure awareness can draw us into a purifying silence. It empties us at the heart, refines us, polishes us up somehow, and makes us smarter. This is the loveliness of a daily activity that enables us to progressively *be* the truth that we are. To illustrate: a reader wrote to say that while in Paris strolling through the Louvre, he was transfixed by one wall of paintings. He stood for hours, appreciating the art, transformed by beauty: "I lack precise words for what occurred. A wholly organizing, non-verbal experience happened—a peak-experience, on the other side of which I was brighter, more perceptive, and at peace." Beauty is silence of a novel sort, moving us into inner spaces where stillness and intelligence merge. A line of poetry, fog wisps in trees, the touch of our infant's hand on ours—each such delicacy resurrects life. Loveliness mystically lures us back to our inherent harmony, and we feel all's right with our world. Beauty reveals not just reality, but also the unseen grandeur beyond it. Each of us knows this already, and the work-a-day world provides ample opportunity to apply what we know to bring it to life.

A Personal Story

I left public instruction the year after I had taken a year's unpaid sabbatical. I spent part of the moratorium in graduate school and the rest meditating. The latter was life-altering. In silence, I heard what I needed. Faith began to mature. Somehow a definitive vocation unfolded—coherently. The future seemed sunny. Problems weighed less. Not all of this happened simultaneously, but imperceptibly tangible solutions popped into mind. Revealed in quiet moments was a germ of realization—an illuminative sprouting: namely, I would follow my delights, the heart's gladness that won't be denied. I longed to honor joy—not for delight's sake, but for life's. The words of Ralph Waldo Trine helped me grasp the fact that there was a sphere of activity meant expressly for me: "To live our highest in all things that pertain to us, and to lend a hand as best we can to all others for this same end."[2]

Coincidentally, the corporate sphere that had brought quick successes (both material and emotional fulfillments) reinforced that vocational awareness—that sense of longing to live my "highest" in all that pertains to me and to help others do the same. I am not sure if that's everyone's truth, but it is mine. From grade school on, and through my tenure as a principal, I'd felt discounted when forwarding novel ideas. At home and at work, I upset the status quo. Private industry provided a positive culture shock: Useful ideas were rewarded. I had free rein to apply my imagination to every conceivable project. When things didn't work, as invariably happens, clients still cheered my initiative. What a concept.

These opportunities (and, better yet, the anticipation of positive efforts to come) spotlighted what I'd missed: empathic mentoring of my finest patterns of contribution. Corporate colleagues asked me to give keynote talks at annual off-site conferences and board of directors' meetings. They *wanted* to hear fresh ideas. They circulated my articles and memos, scribbling their thoughts in the margins. Once during my first year of private practice, a deadpan executive summoned me to the president's office. With heart palpitating, I meekly followed him up a grand spiral stairway, imagining I'd made some royal gaffe. Burnished doors swung open on a throng of senior managers who faced me sporting childlike grins. They began applauding, and with a flourish the spokesman presented me with a gift of Baccarat crystal and a bonus check for service "above and beyond." I floated out of the room.

APPRECIATE WHAT WORKS

Amazing encouragements come when least expected, when we're busily engaged elsewhere and looking the other way. That rewarding go-ahead was so unheard of in my background that, awash with gratitude, I sunk that entire first bonus into a self-publishing venture: a state-of-the-art motivational newsletter that I wrote, edited, produced, and distributed as my firm's gift to each employee of each corporate client. It symbolized my vocational tithe and brought a multifold return. The outreach continued as long as those companies retained my firm (in most cases, for years). After each such success, I'd ask myself, "What worked well and why?"

Before long it was obvious that solutions came out of existing conditions—whatever needs doing—so my program designs became integrative to each corporate culture, typically evolving from low-risk pilot programs. (Senior executives who poorly tolerate that incremental unfolding of customized solutions or who distrust innovation simply don't hire me.) In other words, what works is for a client's creative processes to dovetail with mine. Call it a right fit or good chemistry. For optimal outcomes, relatedness and mutual enjoyment of the cocreative fun of entrepreneuring must exist. On the other side of some winning project, I'd realize that seeming flaws—an inability to mask my zeal or describe precisely *how* I'd proceed—attracted certain predictable sorts who didn't need their information delivered in instantly digestible sound bites. Appreciating those clients magnetized others of that ilk. In any case, defining my own brand of success—knowing what it meant to me—involved being honest about certain defects.

Use Limits as Guides

Over time, to protect my energies, I formed a few sacrosanct policies. Here again, supposed limits led me. For instance, I like a simple life. By 1985, I had friends all over the country.

Whenever I'd land in a city, one colleague or another met me at the airport and whisked me off to dinner. Frequently their spouse (and sometimes their children) joined us. We'd catch up on news over a pizza and jointly plan activities for their firm. Although fun, the mix of travel, time changes, and late dinners undermined the reflective routines that had become central to my way of life.

In self-defense, I designed a new policy: No more night meetings, except those explicitly related to business. Even these were to conclude by 8:30 P.M. After putting the policy in writing, I sent it to clients, steeling myself for their objections. Amazingly no one complained. People identified. They, too, wearied of endless rounds of wining, dining, and evenings out. They wanted to spend time at home, with their families. Soon some corporate friends adopted the no-late-dinner habit. That taught me to trust the tactic of using a "flaw" to achieve some aim, rather than fighting against my nature. Perhaps because I have so many foibles, a profusion of strategies ensued.

Eventually I stopped working on Sunday—one of my shrewdest moves. It's completely restorative to rest at least one day a week. The lightbulb about that renewal lit up when I observed a realtor—a Seventh Day Adventist—close his office every Saturday and let his business community know that he didn't answer the phone or do deals on Saturday. He struck me as courageous, since it's one thing to theorize about keeping the Sabbath and quite another to put teeth into the scriptural law, especially if your bread is buttered by weekend work.

That realtor's example mentored me. Now I rarely travel, lecture, write, pay bills, or talk on the phone on Sunday. It's a day reserved for worship, relaxing, and just loafing. One Sunday a CEO sent me an urgent voice-mail message. I faxed back a note: "Sunday is my day of rest. If it's not an emergency, may I phone you tomorrow?" How pleasant to receive his prompt (faxed) response: The matter could easily wait.

The next morning my client phoned with a compliment about my keeping one day free of work, adding that he sorely needed time off. He, too, now reserves most Sundays for church, family, and "just loafing."

Collectively, we've forgotten that our heritage and spiritual life require us to set aside a day for rest and worship. Both the Old and New Testaments teach this. In the Ten Commandments we read: "Remember the Sabbath day, to keep it holy. Six days you shall labor and do all your work, but the seventh day is a Sabbath of the Lord your God; in it you shall not do any work."[3] Wholesome enjoyment is a form of reverence—sincere appreciation, gratitude. Our bracing delights indicate devotion. No matter how pious their words, dour and unhappy people are not worshipful. The film *The Color Purple* amplifies this theme in a scene where two friends, walking through a meadow profuse with violet wildflowers, are communing with beauty. One friend says something like, "It's probably a sin to ignore such glorious color. It must tick God off when we don't appreciate the purple in those flowers." To abide in feelings of reverence—say, for loveliness wherever we find it—is to revive the soul.

The polls report that Americans have traded their leisure time for a mad, scrambled schedule. We take on two and three jobs to keep up with expenses. We sleep poorly and probably not enough. An editor told me recently, "Sufficient, high-quality sleep is arguably the most overlooked and underestimated factor to human health, at least in the U.S." Recently a news feature described a new trend to reduce the hours slept at night so that more hours might be available for work. Anyone caught up in this rat-racy logic forgets that rest regenerates hope and dynamism. A tranquil mind is ordering and puts matters into perspective. At the very least, decent rest sharpens concentrative power.

One day's physical rest is no longer my primary concern. I crave that deep spiritual restoration promised to "all who are weary and heavy-laden."[4] Of course, I mean peace—stillness and receptivity to the subtleties of sacred, imperceptible beauty. Frequently, that stillness asks us to arise early for prayer, meditation, or study. These habits produce profound self-renewal.

To this end, a contemplative life provides my sweetest, most enduring rewards. Ordinary tasks—cooking, weeding, making beds, paying bills—have become centering disciplines, primarily because they are mundane. Executing these chores properly is a meditative art, no different from executing a corporate project with precision. With a right focus, one never really repeats oneself and every task is fresh and new. We need not *do* anything exotic to obtain harmony and unsurpassed meaning. Nothing can touch one who is *being* a centering stillness, for that one stays open to what life wants to express. Most are closed to their life-honoring cues, as Henry Ward Beecher's lines explain: "There are joys which long to be ours. God sends ten thousand truths, which come about like birds seeking inlet; but we are shut up to them, and so they bring us nothing, but sit and sing a while upon the roof, and then fly away."[5]

We can experience a largely silent, worshipful, *and* relational life whether we live alone or among others. The stillness I'm describing is of mind and heart, not outer "form." It cultivates supernatural identifications, lovely enough to restore us and move intellect, senses, and will spontaneously toward the grace of perceptual unity. This is love. And good things follow.

MORATORIUMS IN SILENCE

Hearing of my enjoyment of silence and reflective moratoriums, a friend said, "This sounds like such a lovely, delicious idea. But for most people, it's impractical. They can't take time off from their obligations. Maybe they have small children to care for. Or jobs they don't want to lose. How many of us have the freedom to take a silent retreat or spiritual moratorium?"

Before proposing lengthy moratoriums in silence as everyone's ideal holiday, I'll add that I *earned* my time off and don't present the idea of moratoriums as an entitlement. Furthermore, moratoriums may not be appropriate at every stage of life. At nineteen years of age, do we really *need* time off? After decades of busy days and weighty responsibilities, it's a different story. Then we might yearn to relinquish selected pressures, reorganize our priorities, juggle schedules and finances to pay for the spiritual regeneration we crave. For parents with young children (or for someone holding down three jobs), time off may not be feasible. Young married couples starting careers tell me they take turns doing household chores, thus giving each other gifts of free time. I've met individuals with a house full of children and mountains of debt who stubbornly block out restorative hours on their calendars: They organize time at dawn or dusk each day, week, and quarter for relaxing. Some people sit in their cars for a quiet period. Others don headphones and listen to music. Done mindfully, fly-fishing, singing in a choir, or herb gardening are all forms of meditation that, somehow, deepen wisdom and manage stress.

Couples, good friends, extended family members rarely take full advantage of their companionship. Weekend retreats are offered by centers of almost every faith and can be attended through one's church or synagogue. Unstructured time is a must for spiritual growth and self-awareness, and it's an *investment* in creative effort. Seen that way, we can appreciate why successful corporations spend millions of dollars on off-site meetings. High-powered teams break bread together, plan their next quarter or year, bring in stimulating speakers, and generally raise the level of collective intelligence—away from the daily grind. Executives golf together. They learn and discuss. They relax. Relaxation pumps new energy, commitment, and creative zest back into the individual and therefore renews the business. To a lesser degree, these times represent opportunities for transcendent learnings and dialogue.

GENTLE EXPLORATIONS OF STILLNESS

Consider the spirit of oneness that emanates from the purest sounds: rainfall, church or temple bells, wind chimes, a bird's song. Universally, these sounds affirm life. Certain Baroque selections, hymns, and gospel songs command such profound attention that ultimately some listeners move beyond thought. In *A Way Without Words* I suggest two transcendent musical selections as a means of entering the heart of stillness: *Requiem* by composer and virtuoso organist Maurice Duruflé (1902) and Bach's *Mass in B Minor:*

> Nearly two hundred years ago, a famed Swiss music critic and publisher called Bach's *Mass in B Minor* "the greatest work of music of all ages and all peoples."

A client who knows of my love of music shared the following story of the healing quality of such pieces: He had read, in personal letters between Swiss psychiatrist Carl Jung and writer Hermann Hesse, that Bach's *Mass in B Minor* had special power. Hesse believed that Bach's *Mass,* and also his *St. Matthew Passion* and *St. John Passion,* were divinely inspired works, that if one listened to them long enough and frequently enough, one would come to know God. My experience with both of these works tells me this is so.[6]

The mentor's spirit reminds us of the silence that undergirds all existence. Apprehending that unity pares away the clutter and the distractions of daily life.

Consider, as discussed, our common experience of rest: If we sit quietly, with eyes closed or looking down, our breathing tends to settle. We may realize, "How shallow my breathing was before." After a few moments, we could feel some restitution of calm, notice how refreshing it is to do nothing, or return to a subjective balance. Sitting peacefully—doing nothing for, say, twenty minutes a day, week after week, month after month, year after year—can result in profound regeneration. Interior harmony uncomplicates us, spiritualizes life, and, frees up both innocence and wisdom.

I've known people who have started modest meditation programs and who sit in stillness, observing their breath, for a mere fifteen minutes a day.* Within a couple of years they give up smoking or gravitate to a new, more positive circle of friends.

---

*It's wise not to try *any* meditation or breathing program without first checking with your physician. These can be powerful exercises despite all gentle appearances.

Truth within reorganizes experience, not sitting motionless as a stone.

Worldly (and whirlwind) attainments might have undone me had that same spiritual truth not progressively revealed its attributes—like subjective beauty and harmony—as the unseen good beneath my own definition of success.

The 8th Lesson

SAY YES AND NO CLEARLY

———◆•※•◆———

The needier we are, the less likely we'll attract productive mentors. Saying yes and no clearly builds confidence and rids us of the misconception that we are powerless.

THE GREATER OUR responsibilities, the less we can afford to spin our wheels in mindless activity. Whether we're growing a business or raising a family, others deserve our steady focus. Worried, forgetful people shortchange themselves and their constituents. The benefits of interior silence—so critical to informing us about what's wanted of life—are essential to the grooming of effective leadership. Becoming self-disciplined in the meditative, life-ordering arts makes sense whatever our goal. Learning to say no to lesser opportunities is integral to that program. How many of us have a mentor who embodies and encourages a centering peace?

One stumbling block to a creative stillness is fear: In our anxiety about what others think, we may avoid taking risks for our secret aims. We don't make time for favored leisure pursuits, won't say no to encroachment from controlling others, and inconvenience ourselves rather than disappoint those in authority. Our politeness is well entrenched and counterproductive. We may feel deprived or resentful.

Building self-confidence required me to say yes and no clearly. To *live* well or reinvent myself along meaningful lines meant self-assertion without guilt. Practice made perfect. It also raised helpful questions: Could I speak up for my values? What did I actually feel or want? Saying no required discernment and traveling beyond convention. How, I asked myself, do I choose to exist? From the vantage point of authenticity, what's my life's agenda? Kierkegaard's *Purity of Heart* provided another inquiry: Do I live in such a way that I am clearly and eternally conscious of being an individual?[1] Mulling over that question for a decade or so brought clarity.

Productive mentors help us assess options from an organizing vantage point. Alan Lakein's classic time management question, "What is the best use of my time right now?"[2] seems rich with the mentor's spirit. Lakein's inquiry is disciplining. Asked often enough, it causes many beguiling enchantments to drop away. The more we consider how we use time, the better we use it. My influential clients say they've taught themselves to speak up for a schedule that suits them. Now I do too, having learned by trial and error and by observing those I admire.

A PERSONAL STORY

In 1992 I arranged a second, partial moratorium during which life was wonderfully *un*spectacular. I wrote nonstop, didn't travel, and substituted a fax machine for the phone. I walked miles each day, and spent peaceful hours gardening. With one enriching exception, I attended no spiritual retreats. My sole objective: to increase time spent in silence.

Naturally, while running errands I'd converse with neighbors and merchants, but overall I just spoke less and contemplated more. I define a simple life as incorporating practical, hands-on activity along with reflection. One just responds to the concrete demands of the moment. That discipline alone can introduce a transcendent reality beyond words, logic, or created forms—my ultimate green-light reward.

Isn't this what the Buddhists mean when admonishing us to chop wood and carry water? Quiet, uncomplicated tasks decrease our usual narcissisms while increasing appreciation for the sweetness of everyday life: Time with a trusted friend, solitude, a spell of daydreaming welcome an intuitive wisdom—unitive intelligence, lucid and radical insight. Solitary days stimulate my religious awareness. To paraphrase the metaphysician Laura Sargent, as discord lessens, only one activity is evident: Spirit functioning in a perfect way. Silence seems one avenue to that, illuminative conversion described in John 15, which I interpret as a transcendent mode of *being,* not a theoretical posture about that possibility. After that second moratorium, work and relationships were never the same again. I gained a stronger faith, greater self-reliance, and gutsy, boundary-setting assertion. The latter surprised me.

Around the time my books grew popular, I cut back on travel. Poor timing. Contractually, I'd agreed to tour the United States for several years running to promote newly released works. The tours seemed pointless. I'd had to address popular TV audiences (who didn't read my books) in a detestable sound bite dialect. The last promotion was the irritant that clinched my intent to live along more austere lines, with a schedule somewhat analogous to a monk's. Before that could happen I had to amend old commitments, and that meant a conscious practice of restraint.

First, I altered every contract as it came due (so that no clause undercut the contemplative life I craved). I stopped squandering attention on toxic, manipulative people. Thus came one of the toughest battles of my life: saying no to that false sense of self that indiscriminately chases activity. I'm still cultivating that skill.

"No" Is a Productive Word

It's amazing how easily the word "no" offends and how difficult it can be to utter that one little word. The contracts I recast were typically publisher boilerplates. These usually require authors to assume heavy obligations for marketing a book for the publisher vis-à-vis the mass media—TV, radio, print. I declined social and business get-togethers. A friend rightly observed that our highest service to others comes as we preserve time for whatever we're inwardly summoned to do. Nevertheless, it was a challenge to curb my natural appetite for each crumb of "opportunity" as I said yes and no clearly—not only to others but to myself as well.

It was helpful to read that Thomas Merton felt emotionally divided by opposing pulls. He threw himself into countless pet projects, tended "to do good things to excess," and went "off the rails."[3] Merton longed to live shut up in a hermitage, to achieve mystical union with God through prayerful means. At the same time, he entertained ambitious worldly ideas. Once he planned to travel to Moscow to become what he thought of as a peace hostage. Then he thought he'd take up residence on the head of some United States missile, be a living target and sacrifice for peace. While setting my house of contradictory ambitions in order, I repeatedly reflected on Merton—a superb mentor.

We can stretch as athletes, performers, or leaders in ways that, over the course of a lifetime, cause us harm. We may seek counterfeit rewards. We might want to be superstars for egotistical reasons—to be significant in someone else's eyes. Left unbridled, our ambitions can enhance a false, unhappy life.

Given the dynamic of my corporate practice, by the early 1990s I had accumulated hundreds of thousands of air miles. I wanted to organize my days toward my contemplative tendencies. It was possible (at home and on the road) to consciously scale back meetings, to discipline myself so that conduct brought real spiritual satisfaction. This meant less socializing, more brisk walks wherever I was, rising at dawn (whether in Chicago or California), and hiring freelancers who also wanted harmony in their lives.

MENTORING PARADOX AND PROTOCOLS

Occasionally when scouting for support services (editors, secretaries, graphic artists, and the like), I'm shocked at how emotionally needy some people are. The best of the best suppliers are independent, self-possessed professionals, able to provide a clear-cut service. A few crave personal contact. Some ask to visit me. Others ask me to drive to their locations. Both of these ideas sound extraordinarily time-consuming to me, especially when someone requires explicit guidance with a project. To be productive, it's critical to sidestep the trap of unnecessary meetings or the business lunch. It's said that if we can't set boundaries with our yes and no, then whoever has the most problems will control our time. Most of us know what it means to become an unwilling caretaker of others. We also should know how to hold the inept at bay. (Painter Georgia O'Keeffe, who designed a re-treat home and a mystique that nurtured her privacy and genius, seemed to have understood the value of setting boundaries.) In self-defense, I learned to assess the self-governance of support service candidates. My successful senior clients showed me how.

Heads of corporations screen their job applicants through intermediaries and by phone, employing an admirable discipline of discernment. They're continuously on guard to upgrade what-ever methods shield them from a steady bombardment of inter-ruption. Everyone from mailroom to boardroom wants five minutes of their time. Executive secretaries act as tactful guardians of their calendars. Early on, too polite to be my own gatekeeper, I sought examples of shielding mechanisms and found instruction everywhere, even on television. Gifted artists, inventive types, and monastics with whom I most closely identify were (and still are) superb inspirers.

Viewing a video biography of one multifaceted artist, I heard his business manager say that her chief job was to protect her client's time and self-interests. That lone sentence reversed my habit of accommodating others: The mentor's spirit at work.

In a burst of candor, one of my favorite CEOs said he'd re-tained my firm only after studying my work ethic, firsthand. A masterful protector of his time, privacy, and strategies, he sur-rounds himself with colleagues who support *his* focus. They avoid small talk and discipline themselves to achieve their peak perfor-mance. Admiring him as I do, his example emboldened me to press on with my "just say no" regime even when clingy sorts criticize.

With all the hoopla made about networking, aspiring execu-tives frequently miscalculate the protocol of attracting mentors.

They may sense that their senior manager is harried or preoccupied but ignore the intuition, having failed to grasp the central paradox of mentoring: The needier we are, the *less* likely we'll attract the choicest mentors. Saying yes and no clearly builds confidence and rids us of the misconception that we're powerless saps.

When someone asks, "What then is a first step in getting mentored?" I usually answer:

- Do participate with organizations that mentor.
- Don't crowd those you admire in a starstruck or exploitive manner.
- Find formal groups legitimately chartered to provide professional support.

Associations of CPAs, dentists, truckers, coin collectors, career counselors, and florists meet annually. Their sole purpose is to further members' career and personal advancement. Every conceivable nonprofit foundation assembles panels of exemplary achievers with the same intent: to give workshops and advice to audience members, though perhaps not one-on-one. Some of these talks offer invaluable aid. The YWCA, YMCA, local colleges and universities, athletic, entrepreneurial, and counseling consortiums gather experts offering a smorgasbord of help. And:

- Be a competent researcher.

No one can enter a bookstore today, or log on to the Internet, without being bombarded with data about whatever's wanted. (Before starting my business, I attended *one* weekend workshop at U.S.C.—on entrepreneuring—but have never stopped reading books and articles on the subject.)

To illustrate the burgeoning assistance available to those interested in mentoring is *Mentor & Protegé,* a newsletter that aims to "accelerate your personal and professional development through the art and practice of mentoring." *Mentor & Protegé* reviews books and articles on mentoring. It offers specific coaching techniques and honors excellence in mentoring. In an early issue, founder, publisher, and former magazine editor Maureen Waters revealed that she discovered the importance of mentoring by responding to her own daughters. Waters *re*discovered the art of mentoring one summer when she was the daycare provider for two of her grandchildren: "I should have been working in my office; as a freelancer one's income is in direct proportion to the amount of time one spends in the office writing and querying. But I found myself 'watching' my grandchildren, responding to their needs. Not that the nine-year-old and eleven-year-old needed watching; *it was just that I needed to observe them.*"[4] Waters used her everyday experiences to further dialogue with her grandchildren. (Here, too, her comments reinforce what has been said about learning and the naturalness of two-way exchange.)

After the children viewed *Apollo 13,* Waters inquired who they considered the key character in the film. She explained her own sense that the flight director was most important, and then the children offered their views. Taking her grandchildren to the library, she'd browse through books with them, extending ordinary happenings into valuable teaching (and active listening) sessions. Waters is a mentor at church, a guide to younger coworkers, and a change agent and leader to local pilot programs designed to mentor girls.

She believes that "if girls become strong women, they can have whatever careers they want—or better yet will have the skills to craft the lives they want." She points out the contradiction of educating children into "voiceless individuals" while expecting them to succeed professionally in an era where success depends on teamwork and effective interpersonal relations.[5] To repeat: A first step in finding a mentor is to participate actively with groups that mentor and learn from them.

A second step: Research local organizations—schools, businesses, communities. Which group has successfully structured a trustworthy mentoring program? Who is a receptive human resource professional? Here's the place to ask, "What mentoring opportunities do you offer people who feel a need for one-on-one coaching?"

Third: Related to publisher Waters's remarks, consider becoming a mentor. You may already be guiding others without noticing your expertise. The expression, "If you want a friend, first be a friend," expands the point. Assuming one has a disposition for mentoring and has identified something of value to offer, it's often desirable to work with mentoring organizations as a volunteer who coaches others in a craft or skill.

A universal dictum supports the idea that we gain self-control and personal reliance by giving whatever we want to receive. Rewording a story in *The Wisdom of the Desert Fathers,* it seems a monk's secular brother always needed a handout. The monk gave him food, money, and clothes but soon noticed his brother growing ever more destitute. In confusion, the monk sought help from his spiritual director: "The more I help, the poorer my brother becomes. What shall I do?" The adviser suggested, "Why not reverse matters? Ask *him* to help you." Approaching his secular brother, the monk said, "I need your support. Please bring me a little something the next time you visit." The brother agreed, and the turnabout proceeded. Now the brother prospered, but the monk felt badly for taking what he did not need so he said, "Things are better with me. Shall I help you again?" To which the secular brother replied, "Oh, no. Since I've been helping you, my fortune has shifted. I've become wealthy. I couldn't afford your help."[6]

What we want from others, we first must give. Giving the thing lessens our belief that we don't have it and are lacking. As we cheerfully devote to others our time, skill, compassion, and friendship—anything worthwhile we *think* we need—the deficit dissolves, and we gain more abundantly in that same sphere.

SAYING YES TO LIFE

There is a giving *to life* that expands us and extinguishes false beliefs. I said yes to that giving during that second year off by creating a modest spiritual retreat at home. The loveliness of a contemplative life summoned me to experience more profoundly that silence I'd come to know as ultimate Reality.

It was a grand year. I scrubbed floors on my hands and knees (as I'd done earlier in life when less busy), planted a tea rose garden, and cultivated my Chinese cooking skills. I watched literally hundreds of videos—one year's worth of classic cartoons, vintage melodramas, and old whodunits. The occupation ceased abruptly when enough was enough, but that one year showed me that everything is potentially spiritual, even movies.

Whether watching fine films or sappy, escapist flicks, some-

thing beneficial was transpiring underground, in the deepest re-
cesses of mind. Over the months as I relaxed, repeating motifs
surfaced as viewing patterns. On some subterranean level, I was
actively forming next steps as a writer and artist, busily resonat-
ing with life's unfurling of questions:[7]

- What's worth doing with the balance of my time on earth?
- Have I expressed my truths and values in a sufficiently beautiful way?
- What wants to happen through and as me now, as God's
  will?

Revived energy birthed sturdy bearings. There was much
more worth saying and doing; a bright vision charmed me back
to work. Hindsight proves that whimsy and enchantments also reveal the mentor's spirit. In fact, the only thing that's ever going on
is the advancing epic of the Inmost Storyteller.

PART III

————•◆•————

THE LEADERSHIP
LINKS TO
MENTORING

The 9th Lesson

CONNECT TO KINDRED SPIRITS

———◆◇◆———

Dialogue with others furthers us, as does internal dialogue. Not only a specific person but also the mentor's spirit helps interpret and shape life. In all cases, affinity counts.

LEADERS MENTOR FROM their wholesome spiritual depths. Stillness of being, individualized one-on-one attention, the growth of self-respect and authentic relationships all culture wholeness. That learning involves compassionate relationships. For instance, considering an organization on paper, we may sketch out charts, financial figures, or hierarchical diagrams. These mechanistic scribbles are inert. Without individuals, there's no lifeblood, no energy. Without the affinity of cooperative relationships, ideas and people grow stale. Ask yourself what your corporate or home-town culture means, and you'll frame answers in universal, people terms.

Most managers readily admit to worrying about employees, especially the quality of decision making. They want to work alongside people who are *capable* of exercising mature judgment. Do workers solve or create problems for the company? Do they appreciate customers? Can they communicate new policies and technologies? Do they inform or insult consumer groups? Without well-meaning, articulate employees, tensions escalate into public relations nightmares. Some individuals, feeling offended and entitled to respect, are quick to contact the media about their concerns. They name a company publically and dramatically divulge the sordid details of an episode: They were denied service, discounted, impolitely treated. Perhaps an employee was overlooked for promotion and files a costly class-action suit. Much trouble is avoided by the mentoring of gracious interpersonal skills. Solid, trusting relationships—not edicts—transmit the social values that grease the wheels of commerce.

Observing how the effective people in our sphere treat others—and us—we learn a give-and-take for divergent ideas or notice a habituated courtesy. All sorts of social niceties get inculcated through productive dialogue. What policy manual ever settled an argument between people? (A good idea may be found on those pages, but to *do* good some individual must apply "the good" in concrete terms.)

People might avoid productive dialogue because their observational experience is impoverished. They've neither seen nor heard a convivial exchange. Some fear intimacy, imagining that it entails touchy-feely intrusions or loathsome psychobabble. Intimacy means appropriate self-disclosure and mutually enriching relationship, not cloying proximity to another. Leaders everywhere might well ask themselves

- In twenty-five words or less, what's my interpersonal vision or philosophy?
- In practical terms, how do I put teeth into that vision?
- Who am I coaching in the nuances of my interpersonal philosophy?

- How am I transmitting my highest goals and values to those likeliest to convey these?
- What's the legacy of my leadership to successive generations?

Young executives (and those with management responsibility) require ample individual attention, guidance, at least one trusted confidant with whom they can explore career perplexities. Substantive mentoring entails spiritual and character formation more than training. Time, patience, and perhaps a little discomfort on everyone's part develops the integration from which authentic vision is born. Ineffable depth of character furthers the dialogue that incubates the fine art of influence. That conversation must somehow be personalized, whether within a family, company, or community, and those talks, especially as we feel understood or glean insight, teach us to walk in the range of our own pace and powers of persuasion. The more substantive the dialogue, the greater the probable range of influence that's developed.

Toward Two Tiers of Mentoring

A historical illustration explains the difference between superficial and more substantive mentoring. In the 1800s French royalty placed great emphasis on table etiquette. Kings, queens, and friends of the court entertained explicit biases about what was and wasn't acceptable comportment for guests. One held knife, fork and spoon just so, spoke demurely, used words, gestures, and napkins with delicacy. Guides must have groomed newcomers in manners, and the use of such things as table implements and meal-time talk. One story has it that a monarch observed a dinner guest picking his teeth with a knife point. So repelled by this was the king that he ordered his cutlery maker to design knives with rounded edges, banning knives with sharp tips (as well as the rude guest) from then on. Traditions linger: Corporate heads still spurn the socially inept.

Two or more tiers of mentoring may be in order. One could address organizational manners: How do we accomplish things around here? How do we dress, converse, and participate with one another? How do we handle conflict? How do we conduct ourselves at meetings, business trips, and off-site celebrations? Another tier could speak to deeper, philosophical intent:

- How do we, as influencers, shape our stakeholders' thinking?
- Who, precisely, are our stakeholders?
- What is our reward, promotion, or expansion ethic?
- What factors make us negotiate settlements or merge with other firms?
- What do we, as leaders, think about this or that community issue?

A mentoring dialogue extends every leader's reach as it cements loyalty to the out-of-reach objective. Every decent interchange can motivate, prepare, or breathe life into next generations of leaders. Not only dialogue with others furthers us, but also the dialogue within ourselves. Not only a specific person but also the mentor's *spirit* helps us interpret and shape life. In all cases, affinity counts.

A Personal Story

Impersonal influences, what I've called the mentor's spirit, protected me. As a teenager, I hunted in books, Scripture, art, poetry, music, and film for clarity about a sacred inner image. No person helped. Until my midforties, not one intimate acknowledged a contemplative life as being viable (or appropriate) for anyone, least of all for me. My religious sensibilities seemed a source of awkwardness for friends and family. In fairness, I could not formulate the words for a proper discussion. Unless I raised the subject of religion, it never surfaced. Early circumstances seemed born to be transcended,[1] since only the flesh bears the flesh but what is born of the Spirit is spirit.[2]

Encouragement for a contemplative life arrived during a religious retreat. I'd arranged a week off to attend a monastery in Puget Sound, requesting spiritual guidance in conjunction with the visit. A bright, serene nun was assigned as my director. On the first day, she interviewed me, eyes widening with recognition on hearing my desire to deepen the reflective direction of life. She blurted out, "Why, you have a vocation for a mixed life! That's a blessed life! There's ample time for silence and plenty left over for engaging actively with your community. While you're here, let's talk about how you can enhance that."

Since that isolated, welcomed discussion, I've forged an unceremonious schedule that gives each day its luster. You've seen that a first step involved admitting what I valued: a solitary, meditative life. A second step necessitated acting on what I loved. *Then* came support (which rolls us right back to the relevance of saying yes and no clearly). What is more productive than to willingly separate from whoever and whatever thwarts life?

Once we yield to the verities of being, once *we* honor the dictates of our own interior truth, defining ourselves according to its parameters and choosing its directions, *then* friends, mentors, ideas, and tangible victory follow.

As a case in point: After *Ordinary People As Monks and Mystics* was published, I received mail from theologians and the cloistered religious—Catholic, Quaker, Jewish, and Buddhist readers—as well as the unchurched. Those who wrote aspired to a simpler, monastic life. Or, they lived that way. The noteworthy letters sparked an ongoing, if infrequent, correspondence. These exchanges evolved slowly, politely. The writers, sober and sincere, encouraged me to continue my research. In the late 1980s a letter from a poet, educator—and cloistered nun—stimulated lengthy response. Sister F seemed experientially linked to the growthful realities my works described. We've corresponded ever since.

Sister F radiates compassion and a finely honed, ecumenical spirituality. Full of empathy, her letters uplift. Sometimes she'll send me a taped response to something I've written—stories about her travels, the mundane or newsworthy goings-on at her monastery, or short verses of poetry. Sometimes I'll phone. Whatever Sister F sends me becomes fodder for my religious studies and reflection. Her humility—that is, her ability to speak gently and from the heart—reminds me how puffed up I can be. She not only writes about truth, she lives it. Her living truth mentors me, and that causes me to suggest that the right friends and ideas follow righteous choices.

Years ago, Sister F toured Poland (and took a special side trip to Auschwitz). I impetuously phoned to wish her a bon voyage and tell her how brave I thought she was to travel alone to Europe. It is not easy to leave our protected nests and venture un-escorted to other lands. (I know seasoned corporate veterans who won't ride a municipal bus alone to tour their town's urban sights.) Given her sheltered norm, Sister F's pluck, her voluntary grappling with airports, foreign languages, and currencies, seemed valiant. The moment we started chatting, we found so much to say that I forgot to convey the intended praise.

Sister F's soft-spokenness reminds me of my mother's quiet, refined, intelligently disposed voice. My mother spent her young years in a convent in the days when school authorities had un-limited, spirit-breaking powers. She refused to discuss that ex-perience, and I only assume she hated it or was somehow injured.

Still, from living in a disciplined, prayerful fashion there comes some polishing of manner, some civilities absorbed. The aesthetic bearing I've always admired so much in my mother must, in part, have drawn me to correspond with Sister F. That mutual accord of a shared perceptual reality also sparks new ideas and self-directed growth, and makes me feel there comes a stage in our life and leadership, when indirect, impersonal encourage-ment suffices. Distant dialogue is, at that point, fulfilling.

MORE ABOUT THE MENTORING PARADOX

The less we need up-close-and-personal mentors, the less am-bivalent we tend to be about our healthy instincts and au-tonomous, creative flourishing. This, too, is progressive, as the next chapter suggests. There's a decided time and place (and ad-vantage) to personal coaching. Yet leaders of all sorts receive mentoring (and transmit their ideals) through tapes and letters, through E-mail and teleconferences and every other impersonal means. It wouldn't hurt those who feel professionally adrift and unaided to mull over three elements of the mentoring paradox:

1. The "higher up" in the organization our mentors, the higher their expectations of us (and the more demands we'll need to place *on ourselves*).

2. In all probability, the broader our mentors' responsibilities, the less personal time they'll devote to us.

3. The more emotionally needy we are, the less likely we are to attract top-level, productive mentors. (Our psychic neediness may, in fact, be a turn-off.)

Overall, we'll derive our mentoring from a kinship of *spirit*. Sister F's commitment to live her truth—her perception of oneness—seems heroic. I relate to her and feel blessed to exchange ideas with someone who loves God and contemplative simplicity and who empathizes with my ardor for such ephemeral things.

Our long-distance rapport is a comfort and an enrichment. It illustrates the way the mentor's spirit works and underscores the value of connecting to kindred spirits—wherever they are. Or as an old line of graffiti has it, "Daisies of the world unite, you have nothing to lose but your chains."[3]

The 10th Lesson

DEVELOP SPIRITUAL INTELLIGENCE

———◆◆◆◆◆———

When we flourish outwardly as sturdy, distinctive persons, we're spiritually intelligent. Spiritual intelligence is our psychic fingerprint as well as an individuated peek into the oneness of things.

EXECUTIVES WHO SENSE a discrepancy between their potentials and their careers are perfect candidates for spiritual work. Aspiring young leaders, in particular, owe it to themselves to develop a broad conceptual framework about spirituality. When shouldering the calculated risks their functions demand, they may wonder what variables to examine.

Various considerations can sidetrack us in youth. Career, financial, or romantic opportunities invite self-testing. Soon after graduation, men and women commonly wonder, "How far can I go, how much can I accomplish with the resources I have? What's worth risking my all for?" Unless they know why they're taking chances—leaving one job for another, marrying this person and not the other, investing in one style of life over another—they can hurl themselves into a dizzying round of pointless, unproductive change.

Here, too, high-trust dialogue about choice and an observational discipline is productive. Independently we can study ordinary heroes and heroines—in film, literature, or real life.

Biographies provide a powerful imagery for structuring superior standards of conduct and life directions.

There is a clear link between mentoring and the unleashing of leadership power. New managers frequently experience self-doubts when needing to control their work team's outcomes. Yet early in a career nothing is more natural than wanting control over results. Mentors can help protégés notice their cultural programming: Have they learned to be excessively docile? Are they able to say no or do they get pushed around? Or are they bullies? The young, unaware that creativity needs *autonomy* in the sphere of expertise, may thwart their finest impulses. The desire to retain creative control over work is often a sign that one is tending toward self-actualization. Shaping outcomes, carving out privacy, or protecting independence are elementary aims of inventive sorts.

Discussions about these issues ameliorate the nearly constant pressure to conform and can draw out an individual's most enduring archetypes or reveal a crippling self-doubt. Both dialogue and self-reflection help us rationally assimilate whatever's occurring.

I rarely meet executives who, privately, don't express a craving for greater decency or competence, or who merely want some increase in personal completion. They sense connections between their emotional integration and their integrity or reach of influence. The more self-aware, the more potency and range of direction they have. The impulse for self-improvement is driven by the soul's awakening and eagerness for unity.

There is a correlation between leadership and spiritual maturity. For instance, emotional stability, willingness to achieve what's valued, clarity of mind and vision, execution and follow-through capabilities are all, in the main, *spiritual* qualities—

virtues. Counselors, educators, healers, and the clergy can help-fully further these discussions *if* they themselves demonstrate what's possible and are congruent. In the safety of reliable, liber-ating conversations, people speak life into their dreams.

If we can frame these subjects nonintrusively, the inherent ac-tivating health present within the other displays itself. Whole-some dialogue spontaneously quickens our will to choose the good. With a trusted friend we can admit our cowardice, then promptly feel our courage rising, sense the lessening of fear. This phenomenon of experiencing our virtue within safe contexts is born of *spiritual intelligence:* an intrinsic brightness that stimu-lates healthy, elegant choices and leads to an upgraded trajectory of conduct. As spiritual intelligence increases, so does healthy in-dependence; conscious choices improve, and we become more willingly accountable for our acts.

A single, truthful conversation, wherein each speaks to the other openly, is usually sufficient to release some individuated brightness, some life-affirming energy. That's why dialogue sparks the mentor's spirit: It releases our soul's song of life, the poetic note that celebrates eternal purposes.

Our small, still voice (precisely as described in Scripture) *is* the mentor's spirit. In fact, whatever resonates with that spiritual truth will further us as individuals. Along this note, I rarely con-cern myself with tidy, antiseptic mentoring techniques spun out by tidy, antiseptic minds (where, for instance, corporations match junior employees with senior managers like a computer dating service). It seems optimally transforming to executives' develop-ment if they simply learn to *hear* the mentor's spirit. That in-cludes learning to trust their own delights, their best thinking, disciplining and inspiring themselves along authentic vocational paths. (Anyone able to accomplish all that tends to become a mentor—if only in spirit—by virtue of potent contributions, enviable productivity, and genuineness. No minor achievement.)

We have seen that inward listening, truthful dialogue, and transcendent moments revitalize us. We may also discover that a sweet growth flows from the spirit of our life's story at its noblest. Rudimentary self-inquiries promote these memories and an inner dialogue:

- When have I lived full-out, and what does that phrase mean to me?
- In retrospect, what's been worth doing?
- In the past, what choices or thoughts have renewed my hope and energy?
- What actions have I taken to live by my own lights? How did that feel?
- As a youngster, what did God's will or my own highest destiny mean to me?
- How often have I *felt* like affirming or saying no to some opportunity but said yes? What does my pattern of response tell me?

Over time, our own answers open our spiritual eyes. Insight, too, is born of spiritual intelligence.

SPIRITUAL INTELLIGENCE

Spiritual intelligence involves an innate cluster of faculties—our deepest, transpersonal resource, supernatural if you will. Our subjective loveliness injects faith and wisdom into everyday matters. That suggests an additive—progressive—function of normal (not "special") growth. Spiritual intelligence is practical. It is our integrated, concretely helpful mind. When we flourish outwardly as sturdy, distinctive persons, we're spiritually intelligent. For me, spiritual intelligence restores the mind of Christ, alive within.

When I began exploring spiritual intelligence in the late 1980s, it seemed linked to wisdom, not measurable (thank God) by standardized I.Q. tests, as Proverbs informs us:

> When wisdom entereth into thine heart, and
> knowledge is pleasant unto thy soul,
> Discretion shall preserve thee,
> understanding shall keep thee.[1]

Spiritual intelligence is multifaceted, intuitive, both body and feeling knowing—the hunch, discernment, animation at the still point of our essential self. We understand what to do in a matter that, before, stymied us. We comprehend the symmetry or purpose of our life. Some say that fasting or chanting or dancing or wall climbing raises their spiritual intelligence. Others attest to the value of reading Scripture or listening to music. Crafts, like weaving, may cultivate that essential energy. Letters cross my desk from those who say that after employing the meditative reading model outlined in *A Way Without Words,* their lives markedly improved. In pursuit of wisdom we can ask ourselves: "What brings me to life?" Spiritual intelligence is our psychic fingerprint, as well as an individuated peek into the oneness of things.

Healthy choosers intuitively cultivate their spiritual intelligence (whatever they name it). Above all, these individuals trust an internal compass and conduct their lives from a self-directed reason that, at times, can seem illogical. One woman nearing retirement quit her administrative position to join the Peace Corps. Her friends thought it made no sense to leave a secure, well-paying position for a new job as a teacher in a one-room schoolhouse on a tiny South Sea island. Then they learned she'd always longed to work for the Peace Corps. It took her years to appreciate the deeper symmetry of that desire, and years more to summon the courage to join. Understanding our life's unique design, its beauty and inherent wisdoms, comes slowly and only with discernment. The question is: Have we opened our mind to welcome in a piercing spiritual intelligence, and, as G. K. Chesterton wondered, have we shut it again on something truly valuable and solid?[2]

In 1983, scholar Howard Gardner proposed that our mind is "composed of a number of semiautonomous intelligences, each with its own separate capacities and developmental trajectory. The linguistic and the mathematical—logical intelligences—are the two assessed by the I.Q. test, though the test doesn't gauge even these two intelligences completely."[3] Gardner itemized at least *five* other intelligences, "almost totally ignored by mainstream psychologists: musical, spatial, bodily, kinesthetic and interpersonal/intrapersonal intelligence."[4]

Both scholars and laypersons intimately relate to the spiritual faculty. Jung, Maslow, Fromm, Erikson, and others speak of "spiritual intelligence" in diverse, psychoanalytic terms. My readers and audiences (accountants, healthcare workers, artists, and so on) use popular words to identify the identical attribute: vitality, creative intelligence, gut feeling, intuition, life impulse, organizing power, healthy instinct, self-preservation, love of life, love. Whatever goads us into loosening the bonds of conventional reasonableness is ever-present.

Middle-aged executives grieve when they realize they've sacrificed their life (and highest wisdoms) to the dictates of their lowest impulses—fear, egoisms, ultra-aggression. I suggest both therapy and only the gentlest growth tactics to take them through that pain and liberate their spiritual intelligence.* In those with diminished ego strength, drastic or intrusive methods of development—intensive weekend workshops conducted by celebrity gurus promising the moon—can produce an identity crisis. If we've neglected our interior life, highly authoritarian facilitators may exacerbate our despair. By contrast, mild and noncompetitive disciplines such as prayer or meditation and certain physical practices like yoga or tai chi are potent growth tools, yet less confrontational. Along with appropriate guidance, these methods pave the way to incremental but nonetheless significant self-improvement. With responsible guides, such timeless techniques release spiritual health by cultivating the interior dynamic that ultimately *is* prayer, *is* stillness, *is* life-sustaining energy. That principle amplifies God's voice[5] and wisdom. Naturally, with that formation, leadership gifts flourish.

On Spiritual Mentors

One reason young executives don't cultivate the fullness of their leadership potential is that they lack caring, capable mentors who are themselves whole—or, at minimum, superb at their function. A peek at a first-rate performance raises our standards

---

*Even benign self-improvement methods may need to be augmented with regular meetings with competent, trained counselors. All the more so if we are depressed, lack an internal compass, or have been abused. It's never too late to start.

of expectation for ourselves. Moreover, a young person's notions about what is worth living (and dying) for or whom to befriend clarifies only over years—through life experience, triumphs, heartbreak, gains, and loss. As young people observe admirable mentors displaying courage or kindness (or even cowardice and cruelty), as they listen to those around them speak honestly (or lie), they're introduced to themselves and gradually comprehend their purposes or gain discretion. Any relationship with merito-rious associates and with *what* we love, mentors us. Even lessons extracted from our association with scoundrels are valuable, so long as they, too, are expert. As Seneca suggests, "With life as with a play—it matters not how long the action is spun out, but how good the acting is."[6]

Undeniably, career-related or corporate mentoring sharpens vocational clarity. Spiritual mentoring goes one better: It puts us in touch with the completion toward which we strive, a significant feature of which is self-reliance. The young must be willing to learn whatever they need, on their own. That point returns us once more to the paradox of mentoring: The greater our self-reliance and skills of discovery, the likelier it is we'll attract the mentors we admire. To repeat: I'm not proposing we rid our-selves of in-person coaches. That's impossible. We need each other. Plainly put, the height of folly is to fancy we can do and learn everything alone. However, the aim of mentoring is whole-some guidance pointing us in the direction of an interior truth. As with good parents or teachers, our mentors' task is to ease them-selves out of a job.

If our mentors encourage us to stand on our own feet, show us how to be reliably ourselves, to trust ourselves or get some job done—not through them but through our own ingenuity—

they're probably reliable. The abusing, nonproductive mentor tries to control or even brainwash us. Productive mentors insist that their protégés become autonomous, accept the costs and consequences of choices, and generally engage everyone's best thinking in the pursuit of goals. In other words, productive mentors embolden us to grow up—to leave home and make our splendid mark on eternity.

AN ILLUSTRATION OF CREATIVE, SELF-RELIANT GROWTH

A young man, still in his twenties, illustrates the self-reliance of actualizing adults, the independent zest for fulfilling potential. CT joined a marketing group I'd been advising. He brought a humanizing, if also novel, background of mental health counseling to his sales function. Characteristic of the high-talent person I've been describing, CT was a quick study. He had intellectual and emotional depth and performed like his more experienced, considerably older colleagues.

CT defined his meaningful life goals when still in his teens. He felt that these objectives should somehow color his business decisions and quest for success, not vice versa. Apparently he'd been considering the issues of his potential since adolescence. CT's ability to articulate and concentrate on freely chosen themes of growth is typical of fast-track employees and central to nearly all true success. Only the individual knows what will kindle his or her drive and enthusiasms and what will snuff these out. Highly creative people such as CT may suffer intensely when confused about their life's purposes. Moreover, they rarely follow orders blindly or submit to a false worldview. CT said that the unfolding of his talent feels like "trying to find the edge of a ball; one edge makes up the next edge, which makes up the next, and so on. There is no end."

Most of us feel under constant pressure to adjust, yet remain open to the lifetime adventure and stimulation of locating our overarching interests. Identifying our relevant gifts and life themes is critical to fulfillment and lifts us above the mere grabbing for gusto that our mass culture advocates. Now we consider vocation: "How am I summoned to come into my own, as a distinctive person in the context of my life with others?"[7]

We flourish when we watch others grow or become contributively self-expressive as a result of our discussions. Others do not improve because of us. They grow because growth and learning are functions entirely spontaneous to a healthy life. Nevertheless, by engaging in genuine mentoring leaders frequently encounter a fulfilling friendship.

It's gratifying to know ourselves as a source of stewardly help to others. Each intellectually honest exchange generates mutual respect, and mentoring typically enlarges the *mentor's* humanity. Supporting the critical, subjective trust necessary for someone else's growth expands our heart. If we use our blessings (talents, insights, intelligence) to *be* a blessing, we are blessed a hundredfold. In that sense, our giving becomes a receiving—but only as we consciously and freely choose to devote ourselves to the other's well-being. A chance remark, a letter of deserved praise, and rapport all seed the mentor's spirit. The affection behind the encouragement does the trick.

A PERSONAL STORY

My father had a poker buddy whose mentoring spirit improved my lot in life. When my father died, his friend unofficially adopted me. At thirteen I needed a substitute father and must have adopted him, too. He was a trucking entrepreneur who retired at thirty as a self-made man—wealthy, impish, down-to-earth. He loved life and people yet took his marching orders from within. To this day, I've not met a more self-reliant person. He radiated all the spiritual distinctiveness I've been exploring: empathy, playful good humor, scrupulous honesty, a finely tuned internal compass. My friend also lived a well-ordered, reflective life that to some extent I've emulated. I suppose we served each other's purposes. I admired him and he knew it. He admired me and I knew it. (That in itself was life-sustaining, an influence I'll never forget.) He encouraged the deep meanings of my existence and I applauded his. He trusted me with his valued books, and I actually read them. During our walks we'd discuss those books and big ideas. He listened to me, and I heard him. He, childless, and I, parentless, developed a trusted bond, and that stimulus of mutual respect affected a lifetime: I still feel immediate fondness for anyone remotely like my friend—anyone, that is, who's an independent, unabashed lover of life. At the dawn of our friendship, my companion was nearing seventy (or so I fancied). Our relationship taught me to welcome my own age and to befriend young and old alike. It proved that mentoring is a two-way street: intergenerational, transcultural, boundless. Years later as a teacher, those lessons were echoed by my students. Each child I encountered was, in some way, me. Oneness of spirit is a given.

I find potential mentors everywhere, in unlikely, even homely, places. I meet train conductors, fishermen, or waitresses with whom, like old friends, I can just hang out. When traveling I take time to eat in humdrum, out-of-the-way diners nestled on the side streets of remote, dusty towns. Rarely do I meet strangers. Everyone seems familiar. Sipping cups of coffee in simple country stores, one encounters endless streams of gentleness—people of wit and subtle insight whose lavish mentor's spirit is cloaked in ordinary garb. Imperfect to be sure, plain by worldly standards, these individuals shine with fundamental goodness and the light of supernatural love. I say this not to idealize small-town life. Regardless of cultural stratum or education, people everywhere have generously nuanced feelings and potential for self-sacrifice— even saintliness. As the mentor's spirit comes alive in us, so does our potential for being—and seeing—good. No wonder God loves us. No wonder we love God.[8]

Thomas Merton once wrote that our spiritual life begins the moment we realize that we're not the center of the world. Productive mentoring helps us appreciate this, and teaches us what we *are* and what we're *not*. For instance, there are some individuals whom I don't choose to mentor. We're cut from inharmonious cloth. I wish them well, but the rapport so necessary for lively spiritual dialogue is absent. Others are instant friends. Our discussions beget mutual self-worth. We find it easy to be as we are—confident or doubt-ridden, fancy or plain. Friendships stemming from such dialogues seem an effortless give-and-take. In fact, these are the intentional acts by which we fully encounter another.

The 11th Lesson

BECOME A GOOD STEWARD

———◆▸◈◂◆———

Wholesome stewardship is universal, a spontaneous impulse of love that calls us to harmony, our sense of oneness. That movement cannot be forced.

MOST OF US spend adulthood dancing to tunes our parents composed. These scores, spun out in childhood, can run our lives. As mentioned earlier, Eric Berne referred to that programming as a script. Berne believed that we know whether we're going to succeed or fail and how we're expected to feel about others because we've been taught what will happen. In sum, we *learn* how to be, learn what it means to be "someone like me." Eventually we hear a story about "someone like me." Fairy tales, street legends, family stories shared at the dinner table, or myths and movies shed light on our archetypes of truth, our injunctions and the prophecies that make us feel, "That's *me*." Identifying with certain characters and motifs, we sense where we're headed, then spend our lives attempting to bring those directives to pass.[1]

Helping professionals empower us to the extent they are wholesome *re*parenters: These teachers and counselors guide us through growth, change, or crisis only as *they* grow wholesomely. These good stewards support our talent or wish to erase unproductive patterns if they help us rewrite our lives according to healthier dictates. We commonly imagine that only adults can reparent. In truth, a reciprocity of stewardship exists: Our children "reparent" us, and we, at our finest, them: Wholesome stewardship is transgenerational, a spontaneous impulse of a loving nature that calls us—somehow—to harmony, integration, and sense of oneness. That cannot be forced. It may explain why we recoil from some people while drawing close to others.

Good stewards never exploit us for their purposes. They serve our need to grow and tackle challenges, and help us defeat our demons. Of course, we never know in advance if those we turn to for assistance or friendship have our best interests at heart. In classic mentoring relationships, beneficent guides will deprive themselves of an advantage rather than steer us unhelpfully. True mentors see us with eyes of love and can no more lead us astray than they could themselves.

A Personal Story

In response to an invitation to a leadership forum, a reader I'll call AR wrote to me. Over the years a series of intermittent exchanges grew into a professional association, and I came to know AR as someone with a quick, open mind and a sense of fun. A professor and counselor, AR is flexible. She tolerates ambiguity and doesn't seem to box others into rigid categories.

AR appeared to be the sort of good steward I wanted to gather on a board for a nonprofit outreach I'd been planning. The still-evolving nonprofit aims to develop the leadership of capable change agents through long-distance learning and mentoring models.

Many otherwise extraordinary adults—capable, intelligent,

well-meaning—remain perfectly average because of their dependencies. Their wish to remain subordinate to, or receive mentoring by, seemingly well-connected others proves this. To gain a business advantage or a sense of belonging, they tolerate shallow relationships. They seek superficial sponsorship by organizational elders and strive for the "right" political connections so that doors of privilege might magically swing open. Subservient relationships may invite favors, but they do nothing to build self-respect or further leadership skill. An adviser and insightful mentor, AR was one of those contributors who actively guides others (instead of wishfully thinking how comforting it would be to have a mentor).

I've proposed that the young can possess the mentor's spirit. It's possible that both AR's leadership and mentoring spirit were shaped, even advanced, by parenthood. She credits her two children for much of her growth; motherhood expanded her as an individual: "My children are highly eclectic and unique. They've taught me to appreciate the wonderful differences in people. Without them, I might not have embraced my own development. I'm so grateful to them for helping me grow."

Family therapists often tell parents that it's not what they *say*, it's what they are and do in a family that teaches, or imprints, their young. As discussed in Part I, the actions underlying adults' essential being easily contradict their sermons. Being and behavior are what children observe, study, remember. The rule applies to helping professionals and managers as well. For example, both ultrasubmissive and ultra-authoritarian adults are nonproductive mentors. Productive mentors set boundaries—not just for us, but for themselves. AR's autonomy must affect her clients positively, since helping professionals influence others toward such traits as strength and authenticity as they *themselves* actualize these qualities.

An initial task for would-be mentors is to set clear standards for how they'll use their time. They can identify what life lessons they want to share. For example, we might ask ourselves

- What (or who) has taught me lessons that I'd like to pass along to others?
- What legacy might I like to leave?
- What losses or hardships have I endured and what wisdoms have I gleaned from these?
- What sort of persons would I like to mentor?
- What burning issue or ideas drive my life?
- How might I enhance the life of future generations or develop the potential to experience peace, beauty, and the heart of their own truths?
- What are five life lessons I'd like to share?

When asked by what criteria she chooses her disciples, a wizened sage replied that, first, she behaves in a submissive, humble manner: "Immediately I reject the haughty who dismiss me because I've been humble." She added, "I also reject whoever reveres me for my humility." In knowing that she didn't want to work with either the groveling or disdainful, the sage identified a population that she felt would be open to her offerings. In that vein, a mentor can ask, "What specific group do I enjoy being with? What value might I add to and seek from my mentoring relationships?"

My interest in mentoring divergent thinkers and leaders relates to my life's experience. Eric Erikson's notion that we age well when we give of ourselves to the next generation seems pertinent to mentors. Let's be frank and say "This is what I need and want out of mentoring. This is what I'd like to share."

A person like AR may become an educator, a counselor, or positive-change agent as a result of her direct experience. Perhaps she wished to impart courage rather than despair. AR's philosophy is that we—the current crop of adults—are now the world's mentors. "We can't forever be searching for wise others. *We* need to take responsibility for providing guidance, and with proper spiritual development, we want to rise to the occasion." AR admits that she sees much to be improved in society and feels heartened to witness regenerations—in herself, her students, her community. Many of us seem caught up in a search for magic bullets, miracle methods, *the* instant answer. Or we try to solve our existential aloneness by "togetherness," by depending on others.

GOOD STEWARDS ARE PRODUCTIVE

Earlier I acknowledged Erich Fromm's contribution to my thinking about productive mentoring. His ideas seemed to have been formed by boyhood experiences during World War I. Fromm came from a religious Jewish family, but grew up in a Christian neighborhood where he was exposed to anti-Semitism and inevitable isolation. When he was fourteen, the war broke out and a "wave of hatred" for the British swept through Germany. That scared and confused Fromm. Adults he'd admired, who had previously expressed a love of peace, turned into rabid nationalists and young Fromm questioned how humans could so completely reverse their basic loyalties. He found one exception to the war hysteria in his English teacher, whose influence of reason and sanity endured despite the reign of terror: "Here was the voice of sanity and realism in the midst of insane hatred—and it was the voice of a respected and admired teacher! [His words] broke through the crazy pattern of hate and national self-glorification and made me wonder and think, 'How is it possible?' "[2] Productive mentors help us feel related, rooted, less frightened, less alone. These are the good stewards whose compelling drives civilize society. They spruce things up by active involvement with others, not necessarily by conventional do-gooding. In their own way and time, according to their idiosyncratic abilities, a good steward like Rosa Parks, Eudora Welty, or the mayor of your hometown raises awareness about what's decent and possible—just by being real.

Living or dead, real or mythical, the mentor's *spirit* is timeless. That spirit appears to us as heroes and heroines in stories, parables, and films or in community leaders and parents, grandparents and friends. These guides need only whisper a phrase of truth to motivate our growth. They don't need to invite us to Rotary Club breakfasts or introduce us to their well-heeled associates. Impersonal influences have moved me toward a contemplative life, my artist's way, my love of God and life in Christ.

When for example, I read that the artist Ben Shahn struggled to express his haunting, inner image—that he really worked at it—his endeavor linked me to my goals. Shahn articulated a truth I felt. Aspects of his message were transmitted by graphic images: Shahn's art transmuted the merely psychological stuff of my experience into a spiritual communion. I call him a productive mentor because he instilled in me an obligation to pick up my cross, as it were, and uncomplainingly tackle my life's tasks, and accept my challenges as necessary and fitting.

The mentor's spirit urges *my* spirit to search each current and particle of existence for the truth. In the allness of a unified perspective, there is only one spirit, one rejoicing, one success. Reading Paul's First Letter to the Corinthians helped me realize it is God's spirit *in us* that searches all things, explores all mysteries of eternity for light—"even the depths of God." For an artist, that reverential oneness is perhaps most frequently felt as a *receiving* of creative energy, and as Erich Fromm suggests the person "begin[s] to experience himself only in the process of creative response . . . loses himself . . . transcends the boundaries of his own person, and at the very moment when he feels 'I am' he also feels 'I am you,' 'I am one with the whole world.' "[3]

Even blurry, inadequate photographs of Shahn's posters (e.g., *This is Nazi Brutality*) or his mural projects (e.g., *Sacco and Vanzetti*) are sufficiently powerful to draw me into that transcendent allness. His images persuade. As artists, writers, teachers, or parents, we profoundly impress each other's lives by telling our truth calmly, quietly, and with a dignity born of innocent being.

Our spirit searches the world for evidence of that oneness of courage, conviction, and depth, exulting when it hits its mark. Observing such qualities in Shahn's words and art bears instant fruit: I gain a cosmic sense, feel obliged to sacrifice certain commercial pursuits for deeper, if less remunerative, expressions of that same imperishable glory, whatever forms it takes. When disheartened, the mentor's spirit in Shahn's work revives my optimism, corrects my course, and inspires faithfulness to life's intent. My love of experimenting may illustrate what I mean.

I tend to feel my way into goals without prior knowledge of the conventional payoff. At minimum, my creative explorations run anywhere from three to ten years, and represent a reality testing of untried ideas—about learning, business, architecture (another love). I aim to make intelligible my truths, to add some bit of tangible light to ordinary life.[4] Seeming delays, rejections, criticisms, my own fears, apathy, sloth, and dullness, the ups and downs of normal creative cycles add fodder for discouragement. Deprived of reward, the mentor's spirit, from wherever it comes, regenerates my faith, ability to persevere and believe in a goal *as if* it already exists.

By faith, the heart rests in simple trust and simple being. Authentic communion with the spirit of truth sparks that faith. Rather than trust regimented training programs, first let us seek out the mentor's spirit, the good and wholesome steward of our own soul. Let's *be* that. Then we can worry about regimented mentoring methods.

The 12th Lesson

MASTER AN INTUITIVE, CREATIVE FLUENCY

———◆•◆•◆———

Almost any group gathering can turn into a collective of one, a unified field, pure awareness: one richly ordered mind clicking out an endless stream of living answers.

WE'RE FOOLISH TO idealize our mentoring relationships. A mentor is mortal and as such imperfect. The mentor *spirit,* as noted, exists impersonally in and "above" persons, in inanimate influences like art, ideas, and nature. Whether in persons, places, or things, that positive influence conveys the eternality of life itself, and that unbounded truth sways us toward what's good. With the right personal mentor, we'll face relational tensions, talk together about problems and work through them. On the other side of reconciliation, we'll experience a greater trust than before. It's usually not conflict or disappointment that causes problems but our mode of handling them. Relationships that avoid tensions or pretend nothing has happened rarely work. A general rule is that the greater our affinity for someone, the easier it is to resolve seeming conflicts.

Given that, I've wondered if corporations appreciate how productivity could skyrocket if their ancillary staff felt some spark of affinity, some shared collegial values. Advisers and strategists, suppliers and freelance contributors usually work independently of one another. Once in a while, a planning meeting attempts to address that lack of synergy.

It's risky business to assemble strangers (no matter how professional or smart they are) and expect them to spit out viable solutions on command. Much is at stake. A company invests years and costly resources in the outcomes of these meetings. Unless those assembled ride the same wavelength of intelligence and attitude they may pull in opposite directions, resisting each other's insights. Having facilitated an impressive array of independent advisers and staff members, I've witnessed a wide spectrum of effectiveness. The best groups are highly collaborative. From the outset of brainstorming they generate useful strategic imperatives. As mentioned in the last chapter, receptivity to others, a shared outlook, and an intelligent, good-humored fusion of ideas invariably produces transformational outcomes, whatever the issue.

A Personal Story

The added simplicity of life during my second sabbatical measurably reinforced the gains of that first leave, a decade before. A quiet, reflective life overhauled my concentration. By the mid-1980s, I'd arrive at advisory sessions with a relaxed focus. Almost immediately, everyone else relaxed, too, and we'd all enter that fertile state beyond time and space where ideas are creatively electric. Each of us became a catalytic force for good. People cooperated. They suspended judgment about what was being said, creating a free-flowing brainstorming without the artifice of prescripted methods. After my second leave, such creative fluency (known to engineers and systems analysts as positive feedback) flourished as a new norm. Let me describe that.

Almost any gathering can turn into a collective of one, a unified field, pure awareness—one richly ordered mind yielding a profusion of novel answers. As minds soar, someone will clarify a point or accentuate a basic coherency or brighten the group's mood and insight: It's an elegant articulation process, happening *through* us, as a synergistic eloquence that lifts all who are present out of petty concerns into the truth of a practical solution promising to benefit the greater good. We speak of possibilities. We weigh each idea for its long-range potential. We view matters in light of a long-range, corporate vision. In part, we reach C. S. Lewis's World's End where lucidity shines and enchantments cease. Here, it doesn't take genius to notice what must be done. Here, ownership of answers is the norm since everyone contributes to an impersonal, flowing exchange. At best, such teams (i.e., of family, friends, and associates) become fluidly performing, fine-tuned units—ensembles who perform beautifully, with conscious precision and not by chance. "Luck" serves these performers.

Actions resulting from such clarity of the collective mind are generally (not *always*) appropriate. Sometimes they may be superior. This is ordinary if also uncommon. Given the fixed, linear scope of conventional meetings, fuzzy, separated minds can dominate. Generally group members are barely awake. That potential for lethargy exists for any group, yet a Buddhist saying sums up the nearness of our promise: "When people reach their highest condition, it is nothing special—it is their normal state."

In our times of high condition, we can *see* someone's answer much as we might feel our own—in the imagery of his or her speech suggests itself in body and especially in breath. When right answers start flowing, musculature and breathing changes. Someone sighs, or takes in deep breaths of air, or chokes up with emotion. Should anyone stammer while expressing an insight, the unitive awareness within the group takes over, feeds creative thought, and what's meant to be said gets said. Protective blinders fall away. We come into our truths, our breath, our life. This is creative, intuitive fluency.

After such sessions, my clients are often nonplussed. They'll ask openly, "What just happened here?" One senior VP repeatedly marveled, "I've never experienced such ease of thinking before." Shortly after a dialogue session of the high-condition variety, the staid chairman of a Fortune 500 company abruptly stopped me in the hall. Looking grave and sounding characteristically gruff, he expressed satisfaction: "I can't figure out what's happening, but people are motivated. Ideas are hatching. Whatever you're doing, keep it up." I didn't tell him this, but I believe that these meetings are supernatural and, more, that the high condition could be our norm. The way I see it—and I realize not everyone agrees—is that when the Holy Spirit acts in, or through, even one individual, everyone within that person's reach gets blessed, energized, more loving, healed, and creatively fluent, if briefly. Furthermore, I glean from Scripture that when we are blessed in this fashion, it's so that we can *be* a blessing. This, then, is my seminal refrain: We mentor others from the wealth of our interior blessings, actively further their good so they eventually grow strong (or blessed) enough to further someone *else's* good out of their storehouse of good, their talents, their decencies. In that fashion, one selfless, blessed gesture can spark an eternal cascade of good.

Mentors Encourage Through Chaos

In the early 1990s, I had the good fortune to work with a consummate corporate diplomat who typifies the creative fluency of productive mentors. Then the CEO of a new life care community, PM is by training a gerontologist and a counselor. At the time we met, PM had the unenviable responsibility of developing her corporation's life care facility from ground zero. It was her job to set up the operational details (sales, marketing, health care policies, etc.) for both residents and employees *prior* to breaking ground for construction.

First, we worked together in large group communications sessions with the entire core of that quickly expanding management team. These early meetings served as an assessment tool for later strategic planning.

An early disciplining process is essential during the start-up of any firm.[1] I know of no pat formula for accomplishing that. The inception phase of any enterprise is a fertile, exciting, and chaotic stage that can reach treacherous proportions. Every emerging venture experiences a superfluid, uncertain time of months and even years. That pattern will prove typical of twenty-first-century businesses. Many small companies collapse precisely during this initial period of flux when it's turbulent. The high rate of failure explains the old, oft-repeated Chinese curse, "May you live in interesting times." When things are new, they're unknown and answers must often be invented on the spot. Most managers lack practice in creative adaptivity—a phrase that means we can improvise novel, workable solutions that transcend mere "adjusting."

Remember the signs of *productive* mentors:

- They affirm life and further its potential.
- They enter into authentic dialogue because, at heart, they are genuine and emotionally available.
- They set clear boundaries for self-and-other.
- They embody values and virtues others merely extol ("walk the talk").
- They stabilize people in a continuity of effort because they themselves are grounded.

Productive mentors are a boon to any new firm or youthful workforce.

PM's natural dignity brought a much-needed poise to the insecure new venture. Unlike many executives, PM is at home in fast-changing environments. She's well-traveled, has lived and worked abroad, and has experienced numerous personal transitions. Coupled with good judgment, this may account for her ability to take things as they come. She's a manager who mentors others through change. Despite uncertainty, PM appears unruffled. As with other gifted managers, she's open to the circuitous process of improvisation: That's a distinguishing trait of entrepreneurs and a requirment for corporations experiencing non-stop growth. While building an enterprise, PM invents answers for what's needed. She's constant enough within herself to tolerate sudden shifts in direction. She adapts with aplomb, demonstrating creative adaptivity for others not merely by adjusting to given circumstances, but by shaping events in her favor.

PM's friendship with her parents and sons impresses me as unusual and enviable. Her father, a former minister, just celebrated his ninety-fourth birthday. PM's mother lived well into her late eighties. Her sons are young professionals, close with each other, their parents, and their grandparents. PM's professional goals involve creating life care centers free of ageist attitudes. Who better to accomplish that than someone who tangibly *lives* the values she espouses? Again, being influences results.

Our early staff meetings established the team affinity mentioned earlier. That strengthened as trust grew (exactly along the lines I'd observed in my days as a principal). When people sense that critical objectives are being met, they feel victorious, even when their wins involve small tasks. Incidental successes prove that they can clear larger hurdles, thus confidence rises. In a start-up mode, few road maps are available. Continual exploration is the standard. Uneventful successes consciously celebrated can lead to future gains. We used *Developing a 21st Century Mind* and the Positive Structuring model as our text for analyzing team creativity. By now, I was leaning on my body of work for all corporate programs. Moving through the paces of, say, an ambiguous start-up process was made easier with a text others could read (especially one that I had written). PM invested herself in long-term planning and educational sessions, and her flexibility increased everyone's willingness to experiment. Some of our team sessions worked and some didn't. The meetings that "failed" furthered us handsomely. People observed *how* one learns from surprises. Even when on the surface some idea proved worthless, at a deeper level we were structuring an ability to roll with the unexpected punch.

The kindly humor and grace implicit in PM's management style ensure consistent, productive outcomes. Those who mentor others during, and through, times of change must embody the flexibility they extol. If American industry knew how to train leaders in creative adaptivity, it would. But training, as PM once quipped, is what we do with puppies, not people. For profit and self-fulfillment to become workplace norms (instead of exceptions), leadership *development* and generous mentoring are in order.

For Further Reflection

An elderly wife of an elderly farmer once observed that her mother had taught her how to stitch a quilt. When sewing fatigued her, she pressed on, realizing that her farming life had also taught her how to endure. The colors in those quilts, she took full credit for, saying they were hers alone to sew into patterns no one had ever seen before.[2] That insight shows she's an artist, whatever else her ordinary life may communicate to others. Only an artist sees into the truth of herself, encounters something unique, and strives to reveal that in tangible, real-life expressions. Only an artist draws from discernment, a present-centered, intimate oneness with life. Ben Shahn contended that every artist is a thinking, feeling being who is always where life is, namely, here: *"Here* is where life is, the proper setting for creation."[3]

In that vein, my mentors have empowered the artist in me by *being* artists of a sort themselves: By example they've encouraged me to look deep into the thinking, feeling being I am. However, as you've seen, I couldn't possibly confine the mentoring function to people alone. Daily prayer, meditation, the reading of Scripture, listening to music, and a life lived at the edge of a wilderness affirm insights, bring joy and the energy to rebound when discouraged. There are days when only prayer helps, when

I've felt so desolate that God is my sole refuge. I'd also credit a sulfuric meandering—at times quite dull and aimless—a contemplative chewing over of things, as pointing directly to the way I'm fashioned. The more I give in to that "let it be" stance, the better things go. That instinctive snail's pace coaxes out the sweet nuances of revelation. The words of mystic Jacob Boehme frame this for me: "If thou conceivest a small minute circle, as small as a grain of mustard seed, yet the Heart of God is wholly and perfectly therein: and if thou art born in God, then there is in thyself (in the circle of thy life) the whole Heart of God undivided."[4]

Ideas and books and the arts, and the untamed beauty of nature are constant, faithful mentors. Like the elderly quilter, I claim my shades of self (both drab and bright) as mine alone to display in patterns no one has ever seen before, and claim the bent and warp of my core being (however ludicrous or lovely) as mine alone to do with what I sense I must.

And what of others? How might we further their sense of self and oneness, or transmit the mentor's spirit to young and old, to parents, executives, helping professionals—to all those who work with people? I find more questions than answers, and these, too, lead to the good.

How to Further the Mentor's Spirit?

The problem of suppressed creativity in adulthood should make us wonder what sorts of freedoms, hardships, peak experiences, and encouragements have the Steven Spielbergs, the Stevie Wonders, or the Georgia O'Keeffes of the world had *at various stages of life.* What has enabled our creative contributors to transcend society's bias against the bold expression of talent? Why do some people stop contributing at midlife, while others gain and regain power then? Where do our high-functioning creatives go to derive ego strength, their day's energy, their faith to "keep on keepin' on"? Might not the tendency to withdraw, to stop making an effort, be more pronounced in some—like highly creative women—than in others? One accomplished woman, upon hearing my inquiry along these lines, admitted that her heart quickened at the mere mention of gifted women quashing their talents: "Certainly this resonates with my own life. There seems almost an inverse correlation: the more creative, intuitive and mystical the woman, the more the lack of acceptance and not infrequently punitive experiences she has in the world, especially as she attempts to actualize her talents in the traditional organization."

It's time to ask our wholesome good stewards—the effectual, positive change agents among us—about who (and what) motivates *them*. Any group, community, or organization can enter into and facilitate that discussion. What are such people's strategies of self-encouragement? What were they in early childhood? In adolescence? In adulthood? Let's ask everyone, not simply superstars. The patterns of their answers will seed our solutions, particularly if we are gifted, creative types who experience

- isolation (as a result of our ideas or, say, perceptiveness)
- keen sensitivity or ability to empathize
- natural curiosity, a love of discovery
- a tendency to follow hunches and a passion for seeing where intuition leads

- a need to break out of fixed conditions and *re*-create ourselves in the lavish playground of life's unknown

Some say that catering to the mentoring needs of leaders
and the creatively gifted is elitist. To me that response underscores the problem. Those who swim with the current of a mass
mind are accepted easily. They tend to belong, at least superficially. Divergent thinkers are too frequently seen as troublemak-
ers. At times they are annoying. Many zigzag their way to
solutions. The highly creative are prone to playfulness. They ask
disturbing questions and pose irritating, complex answers. This
is an old, tired refrain. It's well known that in classrooms and of-
fices across the country the creatively gifted upset the status quo
by clowning around and exhibiting a preoccupation with their
passions. Whatever their age, most can't stop thinking, can't stop
working (which also means can't stop playing). They don't need
recess or singles bars or Club Med vacations, yet are not worka-
holics (to use a popular, and discounting, buzzword). To the inventive, nothing is more enjoyable than work that courts answers,
that lets them apply their talents, and express their creative
faculties.[5]

Sensitive, alert adults with impressive gifts may bury them,
becoming progressively estranged as they mature. They hide their
abilities, because using them full-out can bring pain. One study
described a group of exceptional engineers who, over time, *withdraw from their own creative potential* in order to avoid criticism
from their peers. Having experienced continual rejection (by
family, friends, management, or work teams), they consciously
repressed their creativity or scientific zeal to skirt attack: being labeled "too brainy," "too preoccupied," "too innovative."

One wonders what trauma caused them to believe that the acceptance of family or associates requires them to sacrifice their gifts. What has taught them that to belong is more valuable than being genuinely who they are?

BLESSED BY THE MENTOR'S SPIRIT

As it turns out, my habit of searching every corner for the mentor's spirit is a blessing. Some, whose job it was to encourage me, lacked mentoring attributes. That no longer matters. Others—faraway friends and wholly impersonal influences—stepped into the breach, and I am grateful. Love is always here, an available and ever-present good that I honor in these pages.

Each fragile undertone and leading of encouragement that has furthered my good has simultaneously turned my attention toward truth—some primal authenticity, some intimate communion with the aspects of being that comprise who I am. I mean to say that the Spirit of truth abides in me, and vice versa, and that Spirit has guided me, as Scripture says, since before Abraham was. Truth alone has power. So I see the mentor's spirit reflected in whatever or whoever helps me demonstrate that truth, the heart's wisdom, whose goal is to *live* the truth. On a universal note, only the law of our authentic being, the law above the law, frees us to be fully ourselves—thinking, feeling individuals with a distinctive, sacred life clamoring for animation at every turn.

That animation is a gift of grace, a vitality seeking outlet in hues and patterns never before seen. Realizing that vitality well, we bear witness to our soul, display life in terms of contribution and unfading comfort—if only by virtue of being real.

For me, the core self is, as Boehme put it, the Heart of God, undivided. For you, it could be something else entirely. Can we simply agree that it's the realizing of Truth that wakes us up? That the truth breaks spells of enchantment and frees us to be who we are. Whereupon—fully present— we sight, shimmering, the World's End.

NOTES

INTRODUCTION

1. C. S. Lewis, *Voyage of the Dawn Treader* (New York: Macmillan, 1952), p. 179.

2. John Muir, *The Story of My Boyhood and Youth* (San Francisco: Sierra Club Books, 1988), pp. ix, 129–130.

3. Peter Browning, ed., *John Muir, In His Own Words* (Lafayette, CA: Great West Books, 1988), p. 21.

4. Browning, *John Muir*, p. 14.

5. Bruce Chatwin, *The Songlines* (New York: Penguin Books, 1987), p. 282.

6. Song of Solomon 8:13.

THE 1ST LESSON

1. Larry Myers, *Training with Cerutty* (Mountain View, CA: World Publications, 1977).

2. *The Oprah Winfrey Show,* 20 May 1997. Burrell's transcript, p. 13–14. © Harpo Productions, Inc.

3. Ibid.

4. Myers, *Training with Cerutty,* p. 29.

5. Marsha Sinetar, *To Build the Life You Want, Create the Work You Love* (New York: St. Martin's Press, 1995).

6. Paraphrased from Anthony deMello, *One Minute Wisdom* (New York: Image Books, 1985).

7. *Larry King Live,* Tina Turner interview, 21 February 1997, Cable News Network Inc. (Fed. Doc. Clearinghouse, Landover, MD 20785), p. 6.

THE 2ND LESSON

1. Bill Russell and Taylor Branch, *Second Wind: The Memoirs of an Opinionated Man* (New York: Ballentine Books, 1979), pp. 41, 43.

2. *The Forbes Scrapbook of Thoughts on the Business of Life* (New York: Forbes, Inc., 1968), p. 52.

3. Malcolm Margolin, *The Way We Lived* (Berkeley, CA: Heyday Books, 1981), p. 95.

4. Linda Kreger Silverman, "Social and Emotional Education of the Gifted," *Roeper Review* 12, no. 3 (March 1990).

5. Ibid., pp. 171–77.

6. deMello, *One Minute Wisdom.*

THE 3RD LESSON

1. Isaiah 30:21.

2. Marsha Sinetar, *Elegant Choices, Healing Choices* (Mahwah, NJ: Paulist Press, 1988).

3. Eli Siegel, *Self and World* (New York: Definition Press, 1981).

4. Abraham Maslow, *Toward a Psychology of Being* (New York: Van Nostrand, 1962), pp. 25–26, for examples.

5. Marsha Sinetar, *Reel Power* (New York: Triumph Books, 1993).

6. John W. Gardner, *Self-Renewal* (New York: Harper, 1971).

THE 4TH LESSON

1. Christopher F. Monte, *Beneath the Mask* (New York: Praeger, 1977), p. 392.

2. Ibid., p. 393. Italics in original.

3. Erich Fromm, *The Art of Loving* (New York: Harper, 1956), p. 121.

4. Garry Wills, *Certain Trumpets* (New York: Simon & Schuster, 1994).

THE 5TH LESSON

1. Marsha Sinetar, *A Way Without Words* (Mahwah, NJ: Paulist Press, 1992), p. 96.

2. Alexander Solzhenitsyn, *Nobel Lecture* (New York: Farrar, Straus & Giroux, 1972), p. 6.

3. Sinetar, *A Way Without Words.*

4. Sinetar, *Elegant Choices, Healing Choices;* Marsha Sinetar, *Developing a 21st Century Mind* (New York: Villard Books, 1991).

5. John D. Morse, ed., *Ben Shahn* (New York: Praeger, 1972), p. 198.

6. Sinetar, *Developing a 21st Century Mind.*

7. St. John of the Cross, *Living Flame of Love* II 9–10, Peers translation, vol. 3, pp. 44–45 in Thomas Merton, *The New Man* (New York: Farrar, Straus & Giroux, 1961), p. 209.

THE 6TH LESSON

1. Psalm 55.21.

2. Max DePree, *Leadership Is an Art* (New York: Dell, 1989), p. 58.

3. Erik Erikson, *Insight and Responsibility* (New York: W. W. Norton, 1964).

THE 7TH LESSON

1. Adapted from deMello, *One Minute Wisdom.*

2. Ralph Waldo Trine, *On the Open Road* (New York: Dodge Publishing, 1908).

3. Exodus 20:8–10.

4. Matthew 11:28.

5. *Forbes Scrapbook of Thoughts on the Business of Life,* p. 191.

6. For the records I've purchased, see Sinetar, *A Way Without Words,* p. 113. Also Bach's *St. Matthew Passion* on Naxos CD (8.553193), featuring the Hungarian Festival Choir of the Hungarian Radio and the Hungarian State Symphony Orchestra, is celestial.

THE 8TH LESSON

1. Soren Kierkegaard, *Purity of Heart* (New York: Harper, 1956), pp. 184–200.

2. Alan Lakein, *How to Get Control of Your Time and Your Life* (New York: New American Library, 1973).

3. Paul Wilkes, ed., *Merton, By Those Who Loved Him* (San Francisco: Harper & Row, 1984), pp. 55, 83.

4. Maureen Waters, "Bruised Shins," *Mentor & Protegé* 7, no. 4 (October 1995), p. 2. Italics added by author. (POB 4382, Overland Park, KS 66204; 913/362-7889)

5. Ibid., p. 3.

6. Sister Benedicta, SLG, *The Wisdom of the Desert Fathers* (Oxford: SLG Press, 1981), p. 43.

7. Sinetar, *Reel Power.*

THE 9TH LESSON

1. Jean Sullivan, *Morning Light* (Mahwah, NJ: Paulist Press, 1976).

2. John 3:6.

3. *Graffiti,* collected by Robert Reisner (New York: Parallax Publishing, 1967), p. 25.

THE 10TH LESSON

1. Proverbs 2:10–11.

2. *Forbes Scrapbook of Thoughts on the Business of Life,* p. 70.

3. John Briggs, *Fire in the Crucible* (Los Angeles: Tarcher, 1990), p. 157.

4. Ibid.

5. Mother Teresa, *Jesus, the Word To Be Spoken* (Ann Arbor, MI: Servant Books, 1986).

6. *Forbes Scrapbook of Thoughts on the Business of Life,* p. 45.

7. Sinetar, *To Build the Life You Want, Create the Work You Love.*

8. Adapted from Rich Heffern interview, "An Ordinary On-going Brightness," *Praying* 62 (September-October 1994): 33, 34.

THE 11TH LESSON

1. Eric Berne, M.D., *What Do You Say After You Say Hello?* (New York: Bantam, 1973), p. 95.

2. Monte, *Beneath the Mask,* p. 383.

3. Quoted in Briggs, *Fire in the Crucible,* p. 80.

4. For a detailed description of the process, see Sinetar, *Developing a 21st Century Mind.*

THE 12TH LESSON

1. See, for example, Paul Hawken, *Growing a Business* (New York: Simon & Schuster, 1987).

2. Patricia Cooper and Norma Bradley Allen, *The Quilters: An Oral History* (New York: Doubleday Anchor Press, 1988), p. 120.

3. Morse, *Ben Shahn,* p. 210.

4. Quoted in Evelyn Underhill, *Mysticism* (New York: Dutton, 1961), p. 100.

5. E. Paul Torrance, *Guiding Creative Talent* (Englewood Cliffs, NJ: Prentice-Hall, 1962).